E-Z PLAY GUITAR

EASY TO READ NOTES WITH TABLATURE

Glorious Hymns

CONTENTS

ISBN 0-634-00689-4

HAL•LEONARD®
CORPORATION

7777 W. BLUEMOUND RD. P.O. BOX 13819 MILWAUKEE, WI 53213

Visit Hal Leonard Online at
www.halleonard.com

STRUM AND PICK PATTERNS

This chart contains the suggested strum and pick patterns that are referred to by number at the beginning of each song in this book. The symbols ⊓ and ∨ in the strum patterns refer to down and up strokes, respectively. The letters in the pick patterns indicate which right-hand fingers plays which strings.

p = thumb
i = index finger
m = middle finger
a = ring finger

For example; Pick Pattern 2
is played: thumb - index - middle - ring

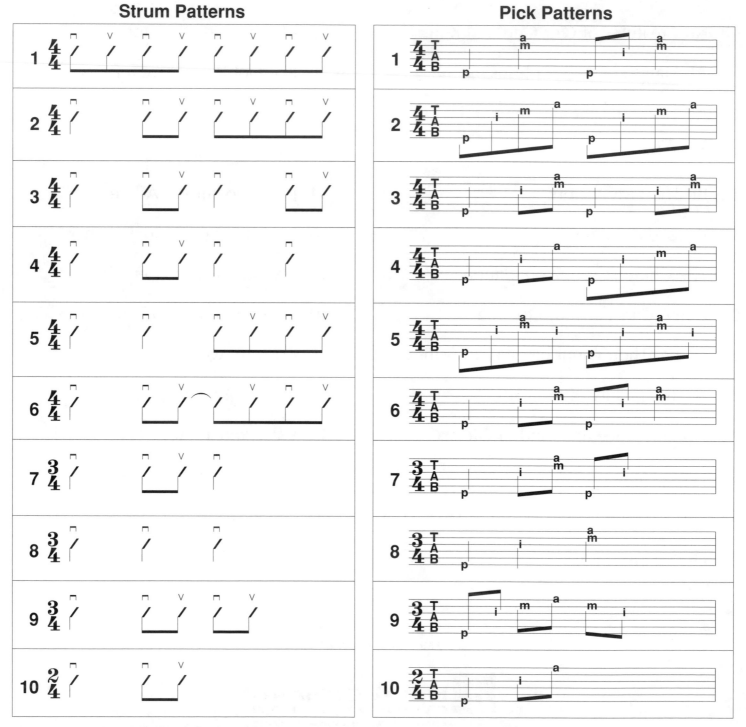

You can use the 3/4 Strum or Pick Patterns in songs written in compound meter (6/8, 9/8, 12/8, etc.).
For example, you can accompany a song in 6/8 by playing the 3/4 pattern twice in each measure.
The 4/4 Strum and Pick Patterns can be used for songs written in cut time (¢) by doubling the note time values in the patterns. Each pattern would therefore last two measures in cut time.

All Creatures of Our God and King

Words by Francis of Assisi
Music from Geistliche Kirchengesang

Strum Pattern: 8
Pick Pattern: 8

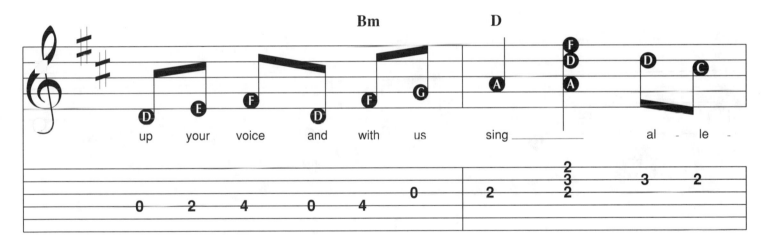

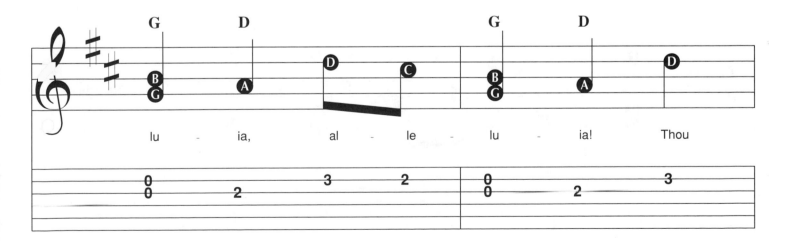

3

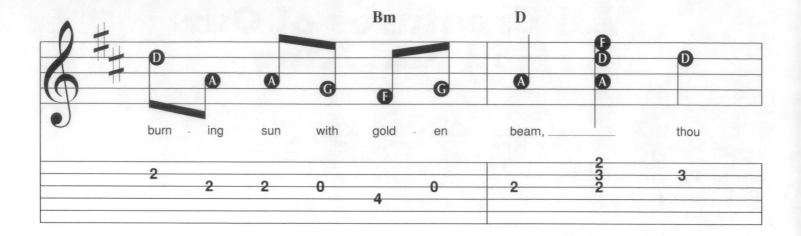

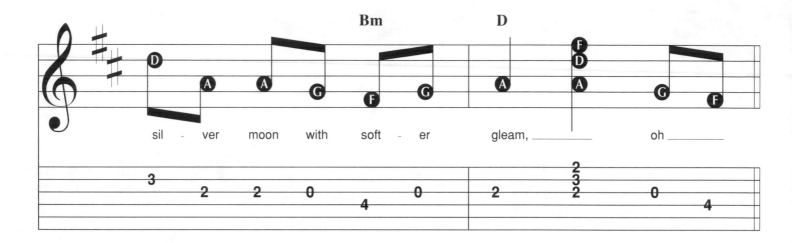

Chorus

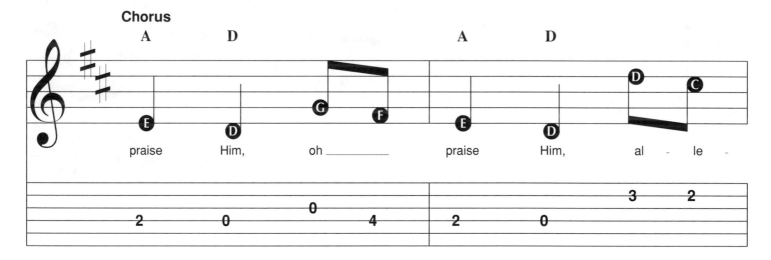

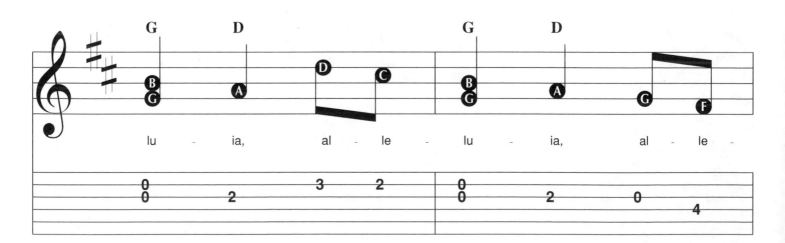

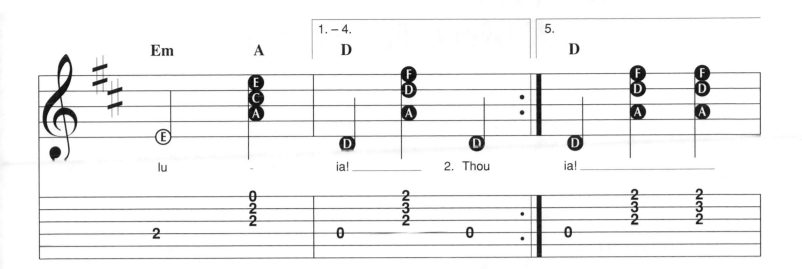

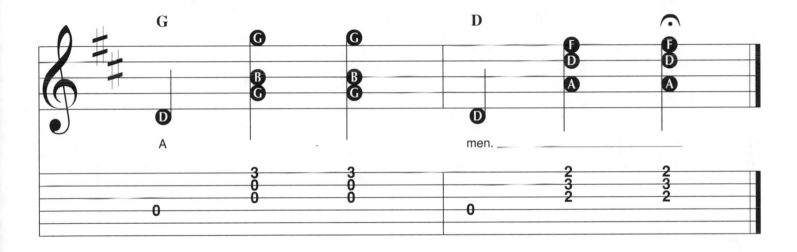

Additional Lyrics

2. Thou rushing wind that art so strong,
   Ye clouds that sail in heav'n along,
   Oh praise Him, alleluia!
   Thou rising morn in praise rejoice,
   Ye lights of evening, find a voice,

3. Thou flowing water, pure and clear,
   Make music for thy Lord to hear,
   Oh praise Him, alleluia!
   Thou fire so masterful and bright,
   That givist man both warmth and light,

4. And all ye men of tender heart,
   Forgiving others, take your part,
   Oh sing ye, alleluia!
   Ye who long pain and sorrow bear,
   Praise God and on Him cast your care,

5. Let all things their Creator bless,
   And worship Him in humbleness,
   Oh praise Him, alleluia!
   Praise, praise the Father, praise the Son,
   And praise the Spirit, three in one,

Abide With Me

Words by Henry F. Lyte
Music by W.H. Monk

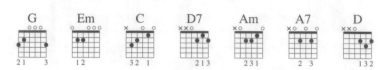

Strum Pattern: 4
Pick Pattern: 5

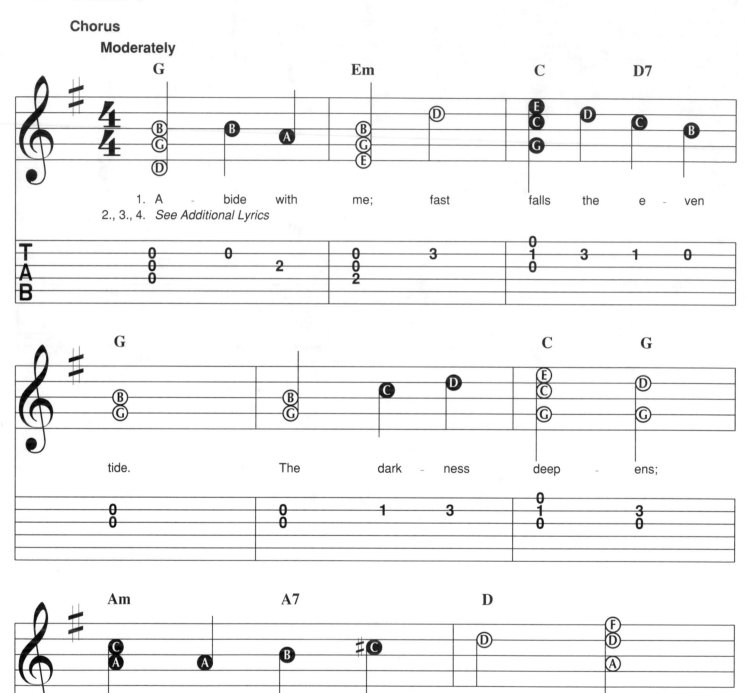

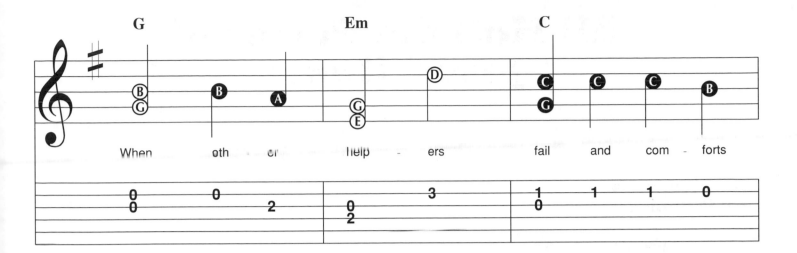

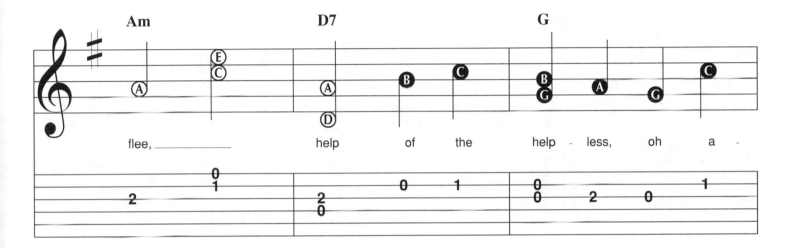

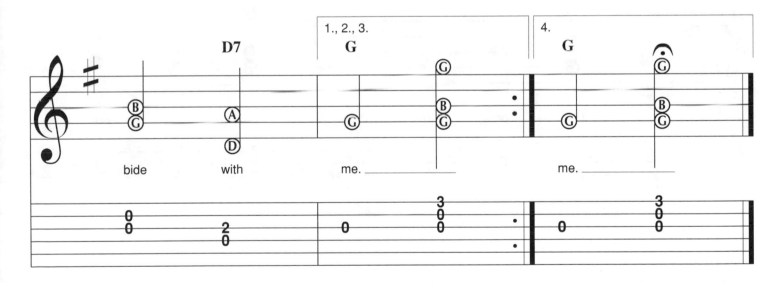

Additional Lyrics

2. Swift to its close ebbs out life's little day.
   Earth's joys grow dim, its glories pass away.
   Change and decay in all around I see.
   Oh, Thou who changest not, abide with me.

3. I need Thy presence every passing hour;
   What but Thy grace can foil the tempter's power?
   Who like Thy self, my guide and stay can be?
   Through cloud and sunshine, Lord, abide with me.

4. I fear no foe with Thee at hand to bless.
   Ills have no weight, and tears no bitterness.
   Where is death's sting? Where, grave, Thy victory?
   I triumph still if Thou abide with me.

All Hail the Power of Jesus' Name

Words by Edward Perronet (v. 1, 3)
Words by John Rippon (v. 2, 4)
Music by James Ellor

Strum Pattern: 4
Pick Pattern: 4

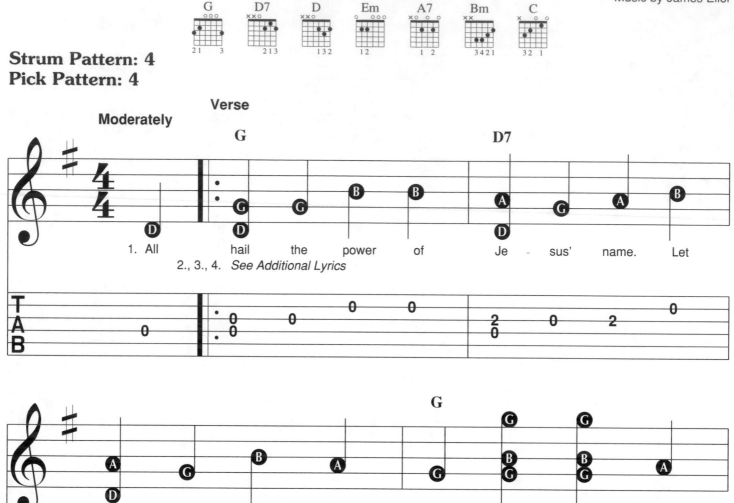

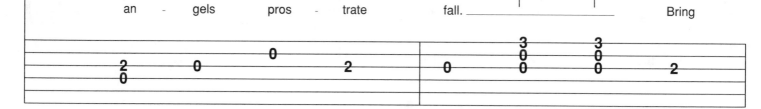

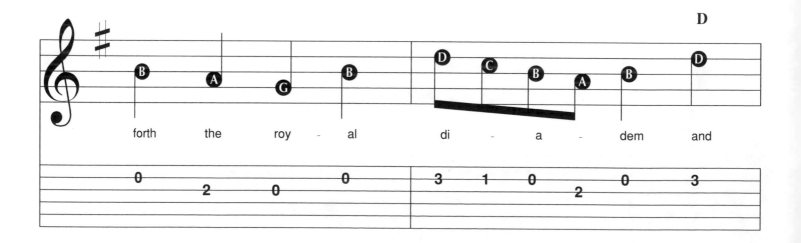

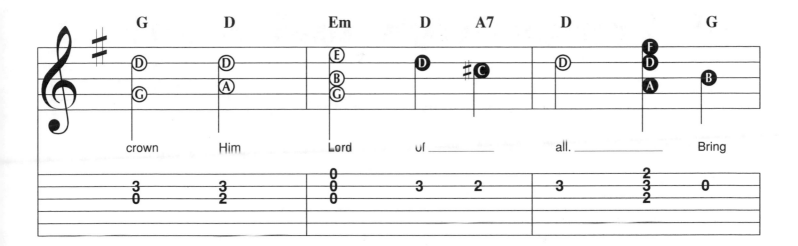

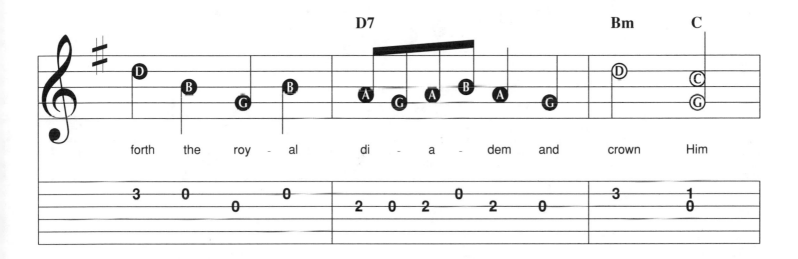

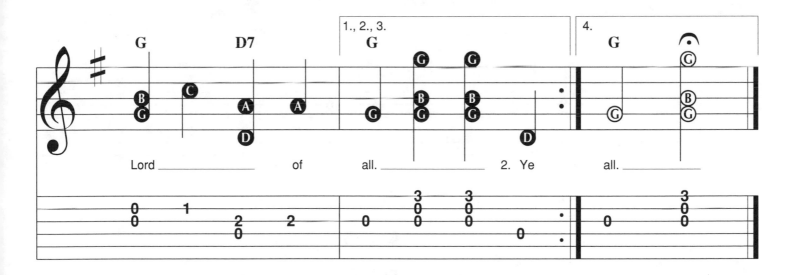

Additional Lyrics

2. Ye chosen seed of Israel's race, ye ransomed from the fall,
Hail Him who saves you by His grace and crown Him Lord of all.
Hail Him who saves you by His grace and crown Him Lord of all.

3. Let ev'ry kindred, ev'ry tribe on this terrestrial ball.
To Him all majesty ascribe and crown Him Lord of all.
To Him all majesty ascribe and crown Him Lord of all.

4. Oh, that with yonder sacred throng we at His feet may fall.
We'll join the everlasting song and crown Him Lord of all.
We'll join the everlasting song and crown Him Lord of all.

All Things Bright and Beautiful

Words by Cecil Frances Alexander
Music by William Henry Monk

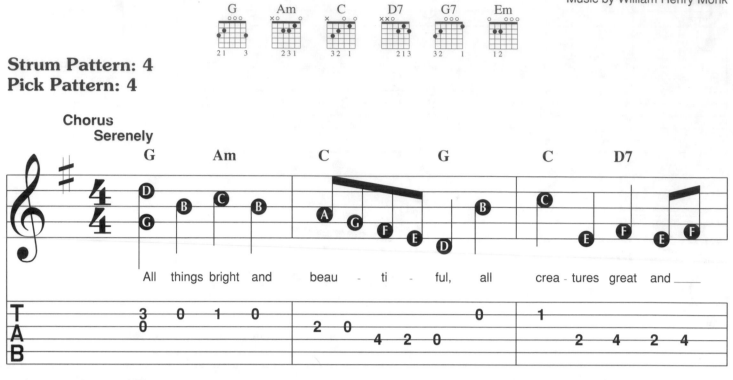

Strum Pattern: 4
Pick Pattern: 4

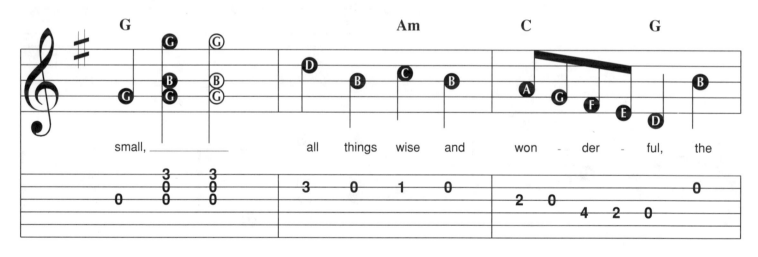

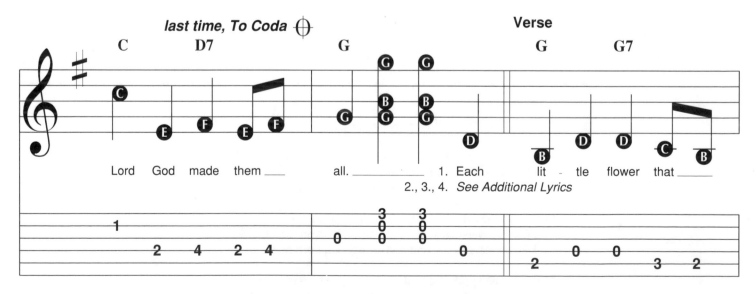

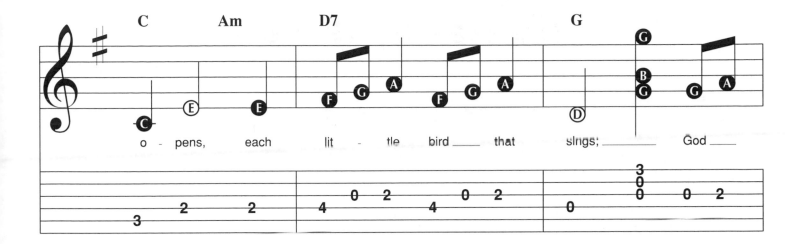

o - pens,   each   lit - tle   bird ____ that   sings; ____ God ____

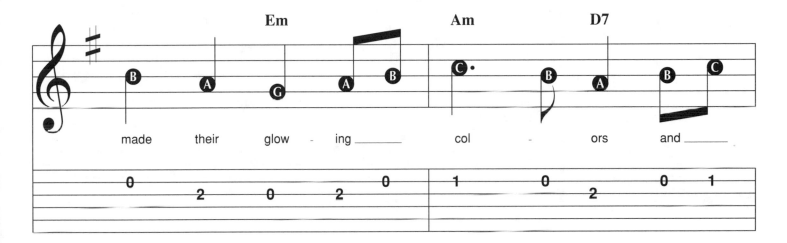

made   their   glow - ing ____ col - ors   and ____

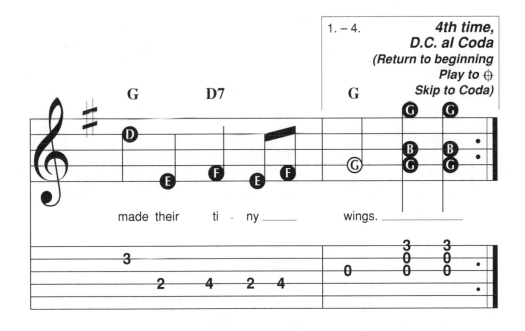

1. – 4.

**4th time,
D.C. al Coda
(Return to beginning
Play to ⊕
Skip to Coda)**

⊕ *Coda*

made their   ti - ny ____ wings. ____

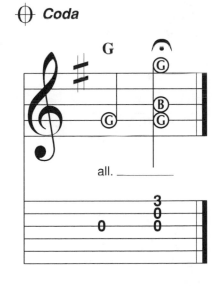

all.

Additional Lyrics

2. The purple headed mountains, the river running by,
   The sunset and the morning that brightens up the sky.

3. The cold wind in the winter, the pleasant summer sun,
   The ripe fruits in the garden; God made them everyone.

4. God gave us eyes to see them, and lips that we might tell
   How great is God almighty, who has made all things well.

Amazing Grace

Words by John Newton
Traditional American Melody

Strum Pattern: 7
Pick Pattern: 7

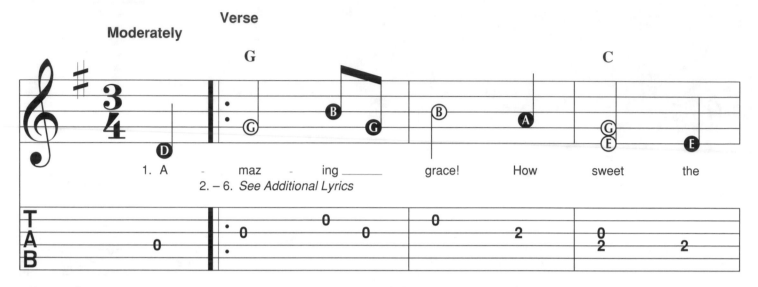

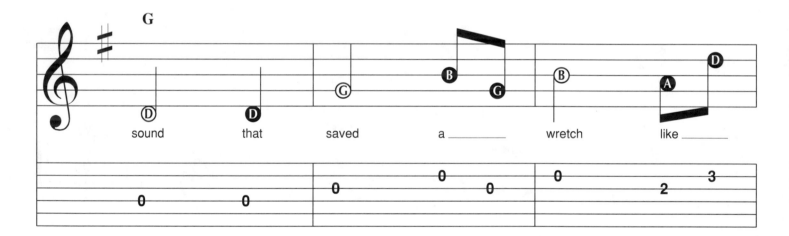

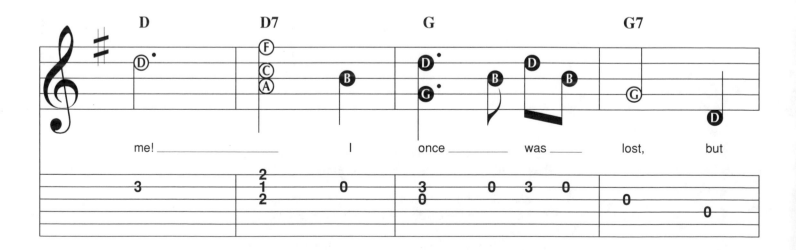

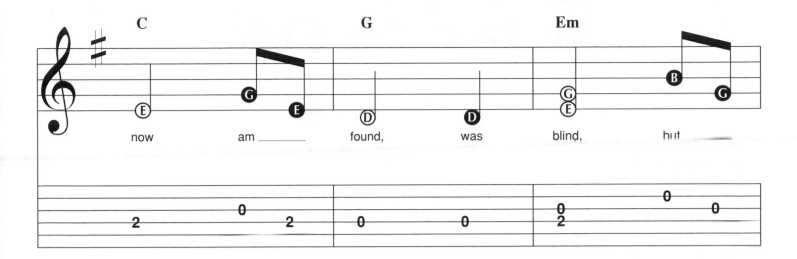

now   am _____ found,   was   blind,   but _____

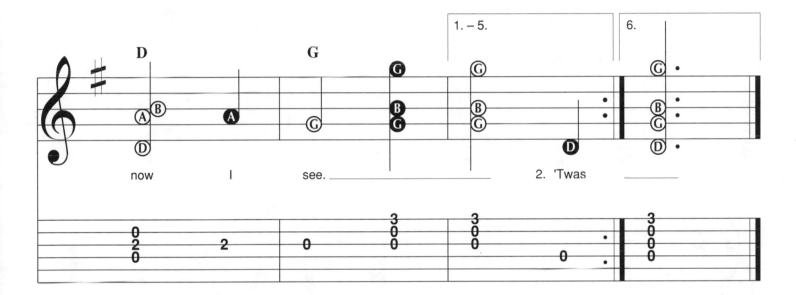

now   I   see. _____   2. 'Twas _____

Additional Lyrics

2. 'Twas grace that taught my heart to fear,
   And grace my fears relieved.
   How precious did that grace appear
   The hour I first believed.

3. Through many dangers, toils and snares,
   I have already come.
   'Tis grace has brought me safe thus far,
   And grace will lead me home.

4. The Lord has promised good to me,
   His word my hope secures.
   He will my shield and portion be
   As long as life endures.

5. And when this flesh and heart shall fail,
   And mortal life shall cease.
   I shall possess within the veil
   A life of joy and peace.

6. When we've been there ten thousand years,
   Bright shining as the sun.
   We've no less days to sing God's praise
   Than when we first begun.

Be Thou My Vision

Traditional Irish

Strum Pattern: 8
Pick Pattern: 8

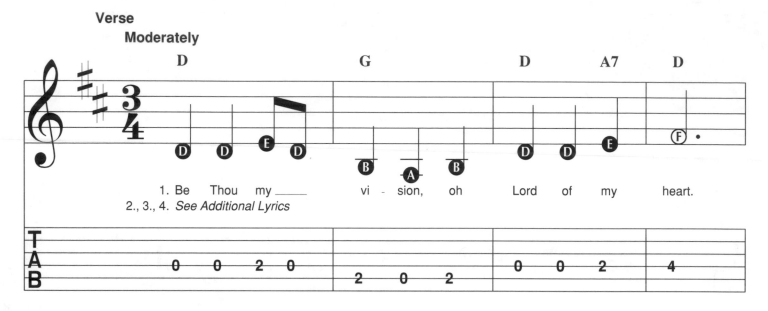

1. Be Thou my _____ vi - sion, oh Lord of my heart.
2., 3., 4. *See Additional Lyrics*

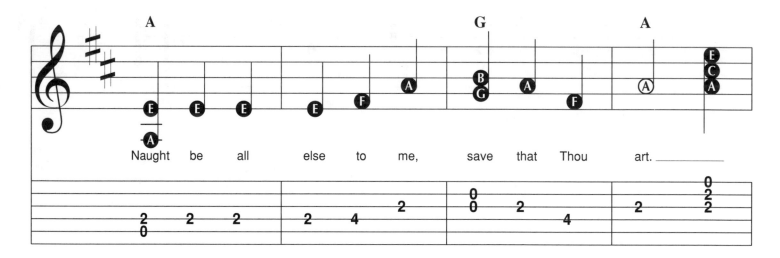

Naught be all else to me, save that Thou art. _____

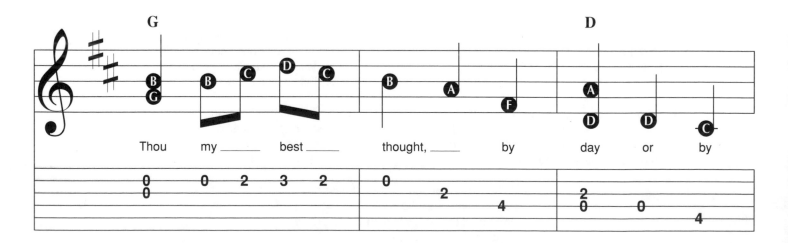

Thou my _____ best _____ thought, _____ by day or by

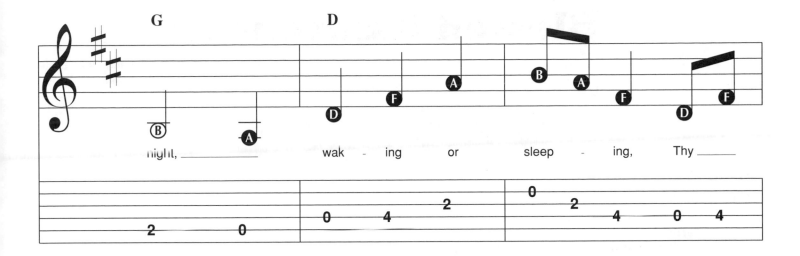

night, _____ wak - ing or sleep - ing, Thy _____

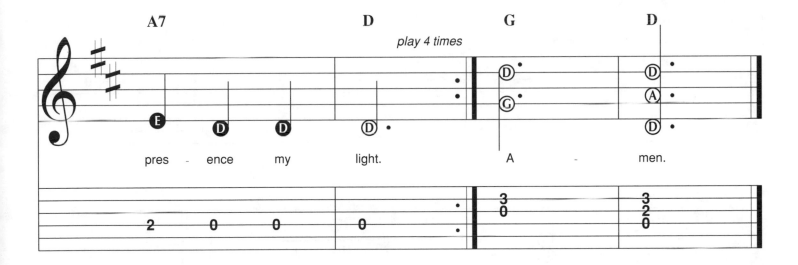

pres - ence my light. A - men.

Additional Lyrics

2. Be Thou my wisdom, and Thou my true word.
   I ever with Thee and Thou with me, Lord.
   Thou my great Father, I Thy true son,
   Thou in me dwelling, and I with Thee one.

3. Riches I heed not, nor man's empty praise.
   Thou mine inheritance, now and always.
   Thou and Thou only, first in my heart,
   High King of heaven, my treasure Thou art.

4. High King of heaven, my victory won.
   May I reach heaven's joys, oh bright heav'n's sun!
   Heart of my own heart, whatever befall,
   Still be my vision, oh Ruler of all.

Blessed Assurance

Lyrics by Fanny Crosby and Van Alstyne
Music by Phoebe P. Knapp

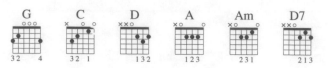

Strum Pattern: 8
Pick Pattern: 8

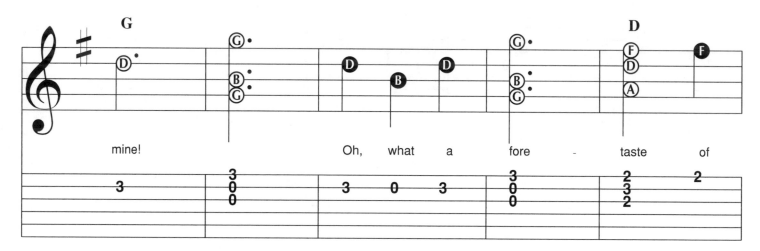

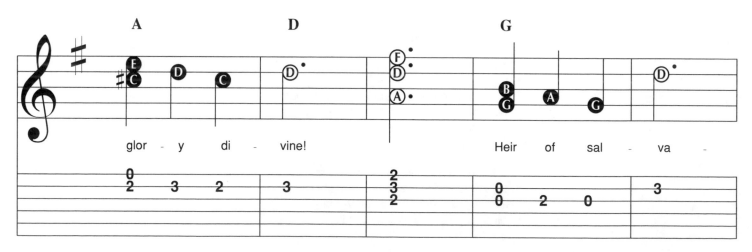

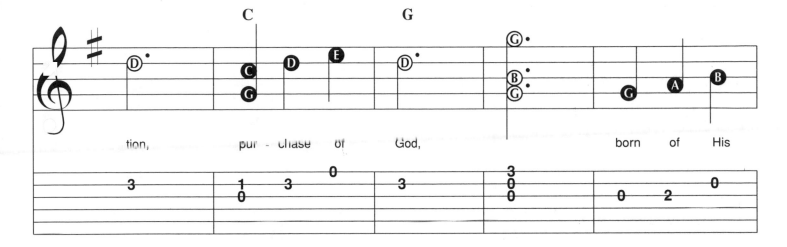

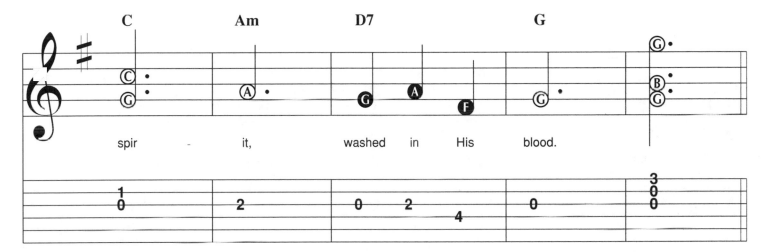

Chorus

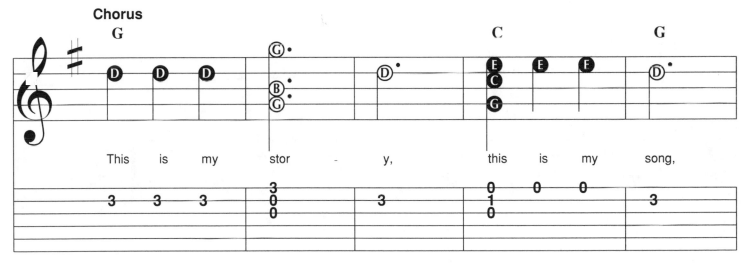

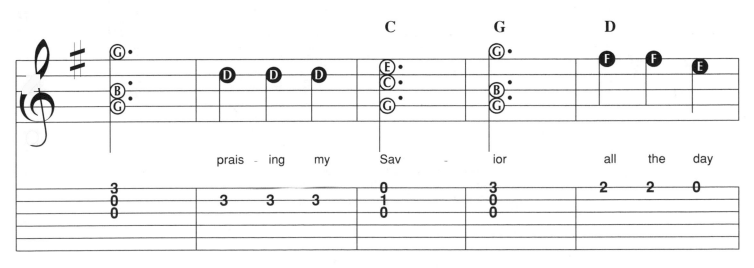

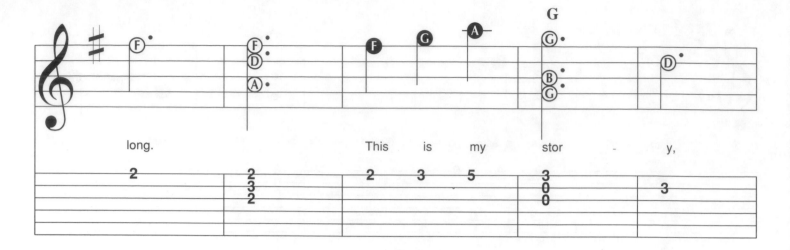

long.   This   is   my   stor -   y,

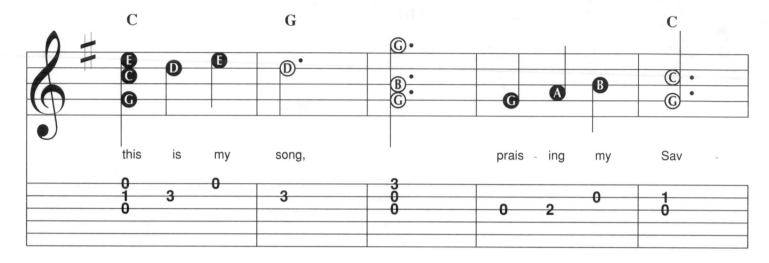

this   is   my   song,   prais - ing   my   Sav -

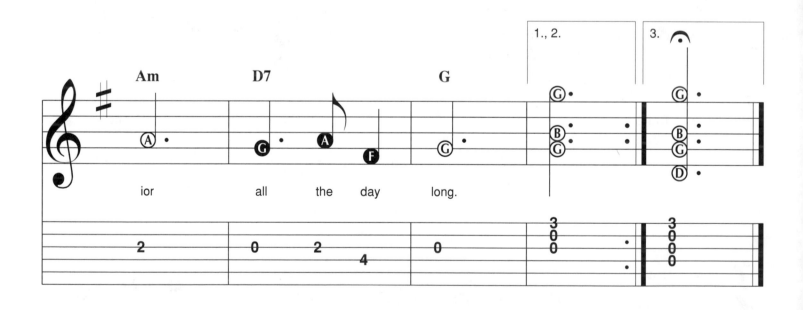

ior   all   the   day   long.

Additional Lyrics

2. Perfect submission, perfect delight,
   Visions of rapture now burst on my sight.
   Angels descending, bring from above
   Echoes of mercy, whispers of love.

3. Perfect submission, all is at rest.
   I in my Savior am happy and blest.
   Watching and waiting, looking above,
   Filled with His goodness, lost in His love.

I Love Thy Kingdom, Lord

Words by Tim Dwight
Music by Aaron Williams

Strum Pattern: 4
Pick Pattern: 4

Verse
Moderately Slow

1. I love thy king - dom, Lord, the house of Thine a -
2., 3. *See Additional Lyrics*

bode. The church our blest re - deem - er saved with

His own pre - cious blood. 2. I end.

Additional Lyrics

2. I love Thy church, oh, God!
Her walls before Thee stand,
Dear as the apple of Thine eye,
And graven on Thy land.

3. For her my tears shall fall,
For her my prayers ascend.
To her my cares and toils be giv'n,
Till toils and cares shall end.

The Church's One Foundation

Words by Samuel Stone
Music by Samuel Wesley

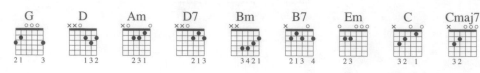

Strum Pattern: 4
Pick Pattern: 1

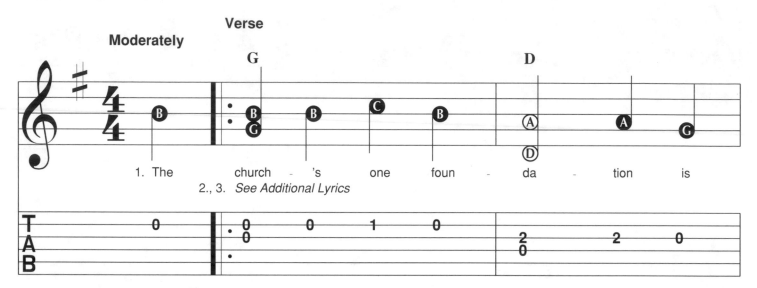

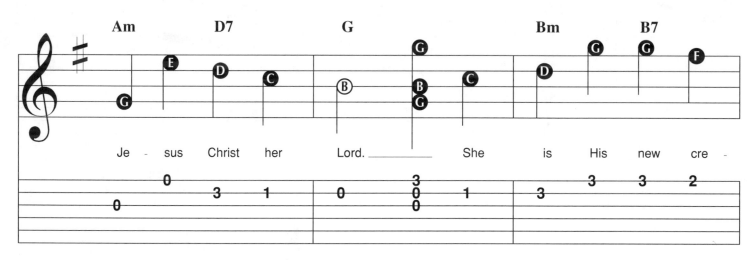

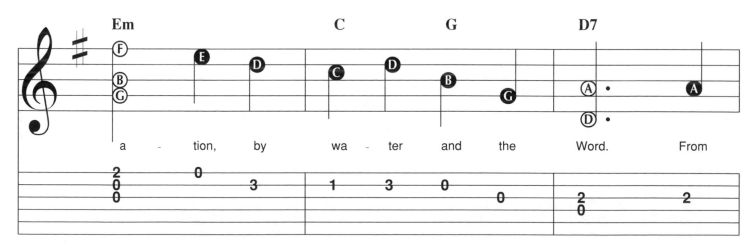

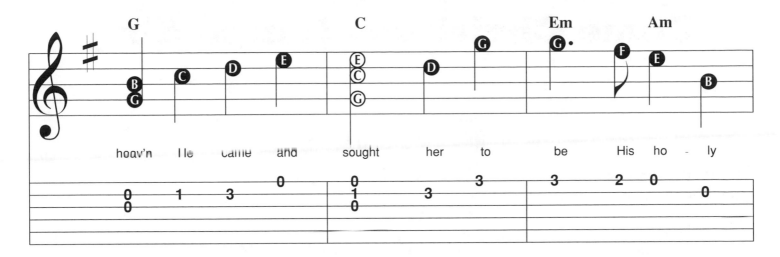

hoav'n He came and sought her to be His ho - ly

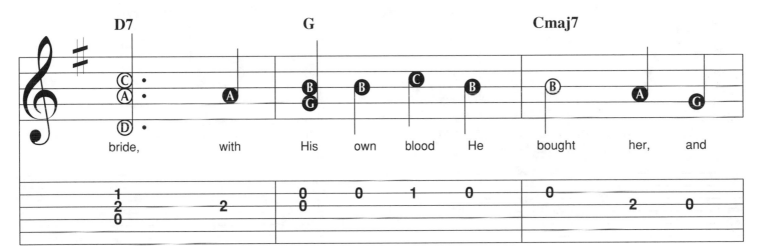

bride, with His own blood He bought her, and

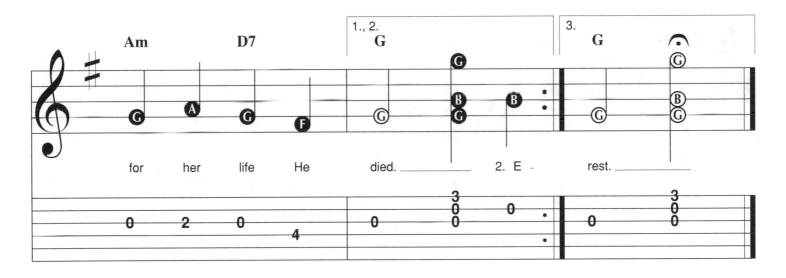

for her life He died. ____ 2. E - rest. ____

Additional Lyrics

2. Elect from ev'ry nation, yet one o'er all the earth.
   Her charter of salvation, one Lord, one faith, one birth.
   One holy name she blesses, partakes one holy food,
   And to one hope she presses, with ev'ry grace endued.

3. 'Mid toil and tribulation, and tumult of her war,
   She waits the consumation of peace forevermore.
   Till with the vision glorious, her longing eyes are blest,
   And the great church victorious shall be the church at rest.

Come Christians Join to Sing

Words by Christian Henry Bateman
Traditional Melody

Strum Pattern: 2
Pick Pattern: 2

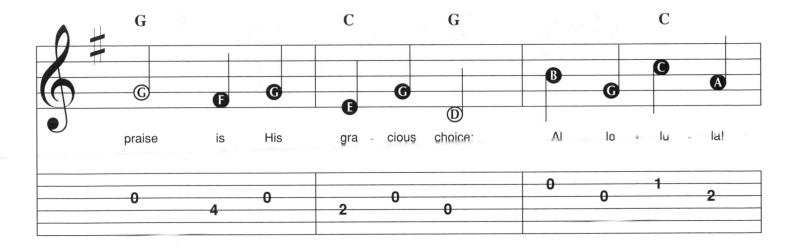

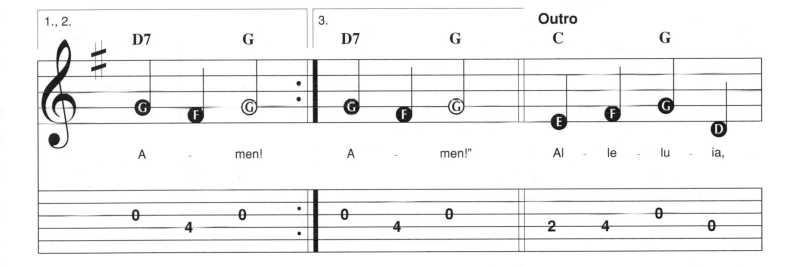

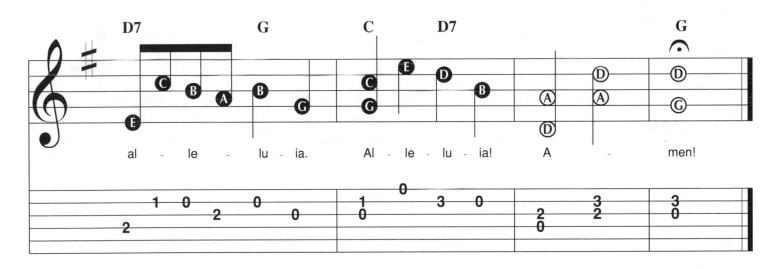

Additional Lyrics

2. Come, lift your hearts on high,
   Alleluia! Amen!
   Let praises fill the sky;
   Alleluia! Amen!
   He is our guide and friend;
   To us He'll condescend;
   His love shall never end:
   Alleluia! Amen!

3. Praise yet our Christ again,
   Alleluia! Amen!
   Life shall not end the strain;
   Alleluia! Amen!
   On heaven's blissful shore
   His goodness we'll adore,
   Singing forevermore,
   "Alleluia! Amen!"

Come, Thou Fount of Every Blessing

Words by Robert Robinson
Traditional Music compiled by John Wyeth

G   D   C

Strum Pattern: 8
Pick Pattern: 8

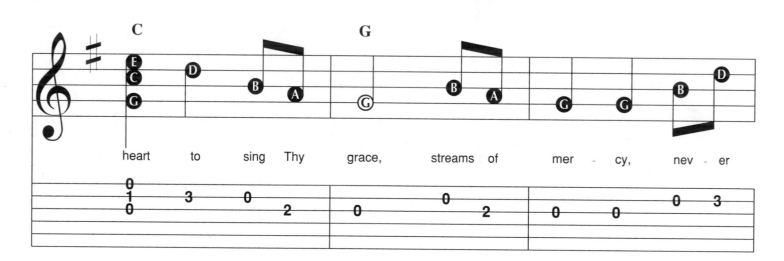

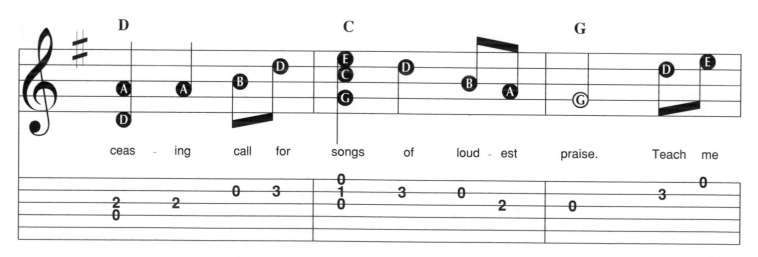

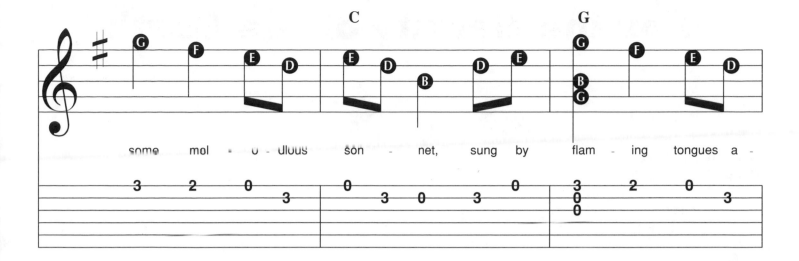

some mel - o - dious son - net, sung by flam - ing tongues a -

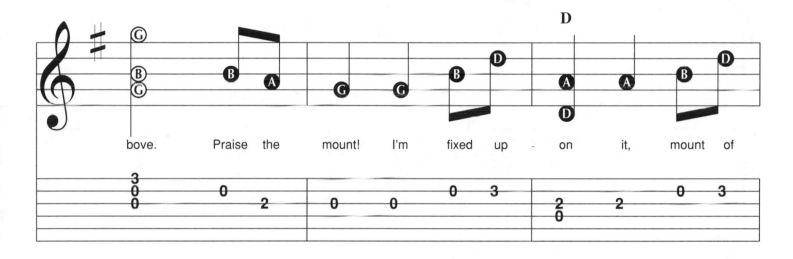

bove. Praise the mount! I'm fixed up - on it, mount of

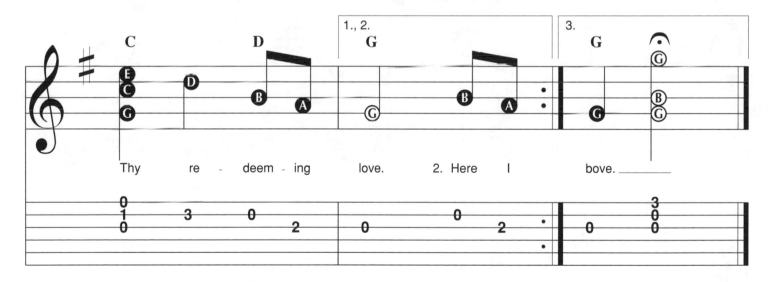

Thy re - deem - ing love. 2. Here I bove._____

Additional Lyrics

2. Here I raise mine Ebenezer,
   Hither by Thy help I'm come.
   And I hope, by Thy good pleasure,
   Safely to arrive at home.
   Jesus sought me when a stranger,
   Wand'ring from the fold of God;
   He, to rescue me from danger,
   Interposed His precious blood.

3. Oh, to grace how great a debtor
   Daily I'm constrained to be!
   Let Thy grace, Lord, like a fetter,
   Bind my wand'ring heart to Thee.
   Prone to wander, Lord I feel it,
   Prone to leave the God I love;
   Here's my heart, Lord, take and seal it,
   Seal it for Thy courts above.

For the Beauty of the Earth

Text by Folliot S. Pierpoint
Music by Conrad Kocher

Strum Pattern: 4
Pick Pattern: 3

Verse

Gently

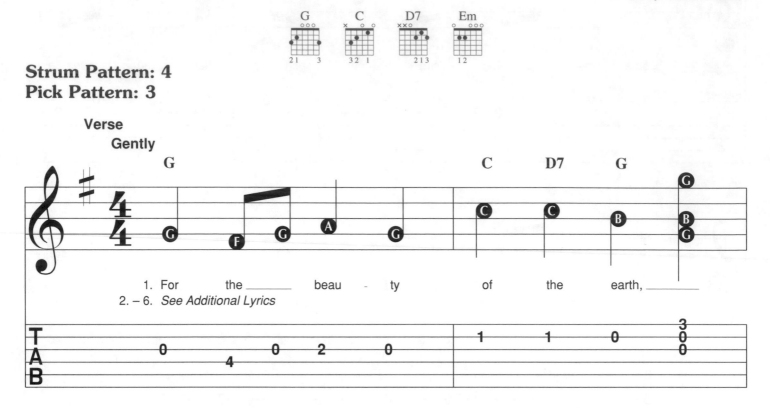

1. For the _____ beau - ty of the earth, _____
2. – 6. *See Additional Lyrics*

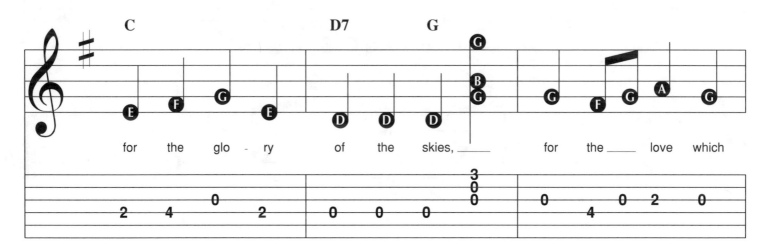

for the glo - ry of the skies, _____ for the _____ love which

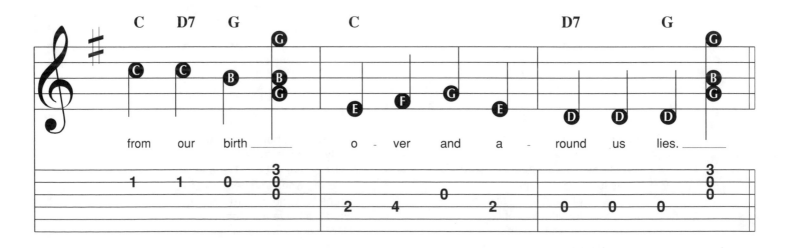

from our birth _____ o - ver and a - round us lies.

Chorus

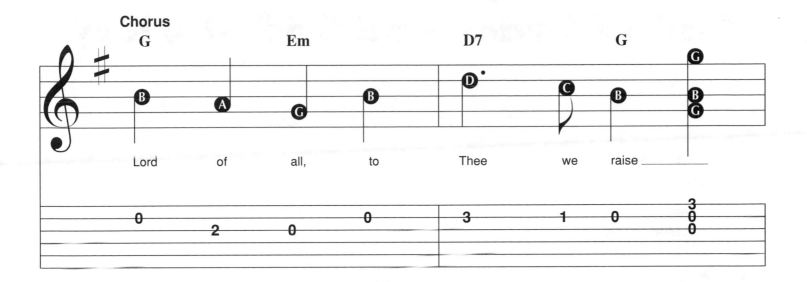

Lord of all, to Thee we raise _____

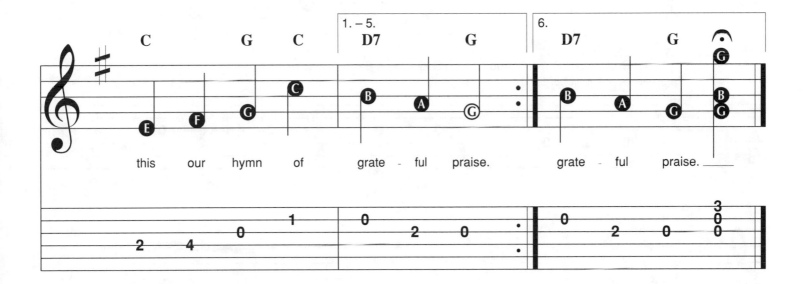

this our hymn of grate - ful praise. grate - ful praise. _____

Additional Lyrics

2. For the beauty of each hour
   Of the day and of the night,
   Hill and vale, and tree and flower,
   Sun and moon and stars of light.

4. For the joy of human love,
   Brother, sister, parent, child,
   Friends on earth and friends above,
   For all gentle thoughts and mild.

6. For Thy self, best Gift Divine,
   To the world so freely given,
   For that great, great love of Thine,
   Peace on earth and joy in heaven.

3. For the joy of ear and eye,
   For the heart and mind's delight,
   For the mystic harmony
   Linking sense to sound and sight.

5. For Thy church that evermore
   Lifteth holy hands above,
   Offering upon every shore
   Her pure sacrifice of love.

Optional Chorus for Holy Communion

Christ, our God, to Thee we raise
This our sacrifice of praise.

God of Grace and God of Glory

Text by Harry Emerson Fosdick
Music by John Hughes

Strum Pattern: 2
Pick Pattern: 2

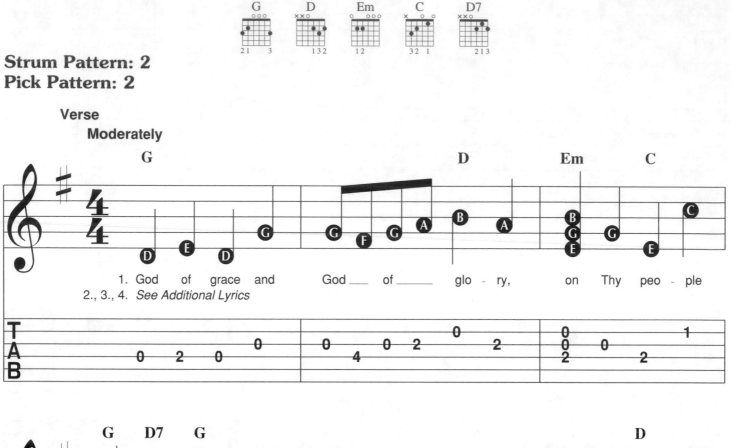

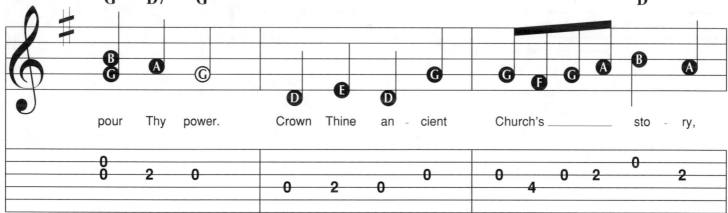

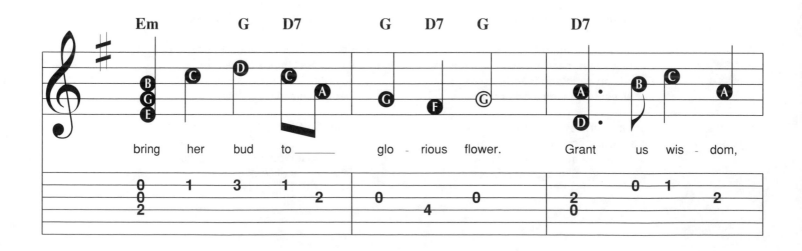

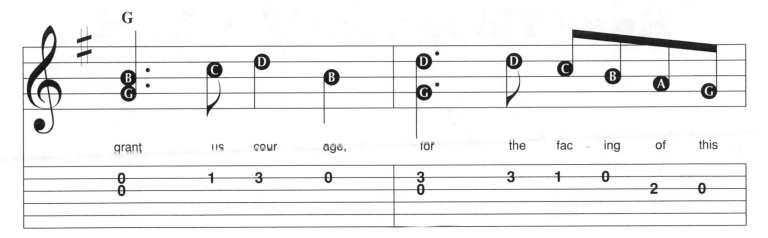

grant   us   cour - age,   for   the   fac - ing   of   this

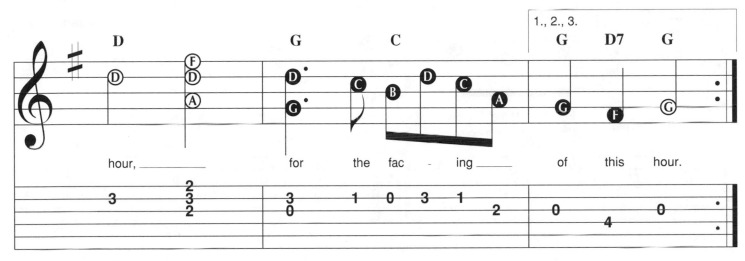

hour, _____   for   the   fac - ing _____   of   this   hour.

Outro

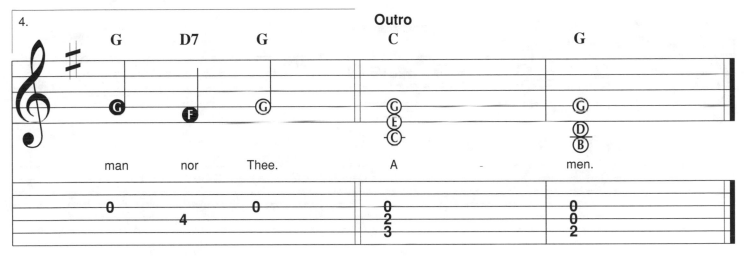

man   nor   Thee.   A   -   men.

Additional Lyrics

2. Lo! The hosts of evil 'round us
Scorn Thy Christ, assail His ways!
From the fears that long have bound us,
Free our hearts to faith and praise.
Grant us wisdom, grant us courage,
For the living of these days,
For the living of these days.

3. Cure Thy children's warring madness,
Bend our pride to Thy control.
Shame our wanton, selfish gladness,
Rich in things and poor in soul.
Grant us wisdom, grant us courage,
Lest we miss Thy Kingdom's goal,
Lest we miss Thy Kingdom's goal.

4. Set our feet on lofty places,
Gird our lives that they may be
Armored with all Christ-like graces
In the fight to set men free.
Grant us wisdom, grant us courage,
That we fail not man nor Thee,
That we fail not man nor Thee.

Have Thine Own Way Lord

Words by Adelaide Pollard
Music by George Stebbins

Strum Pattern: 8
Pick Pattern: 8

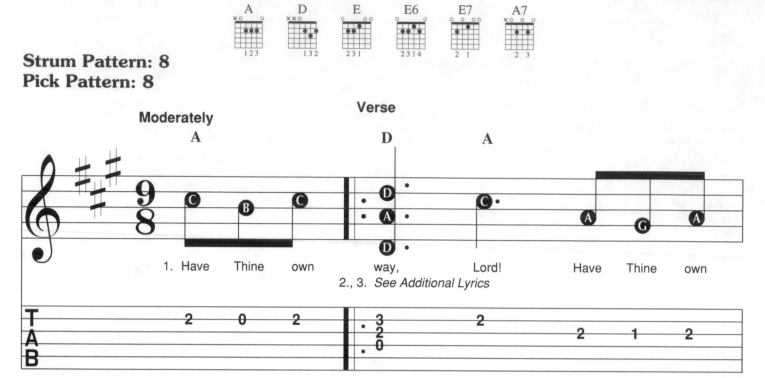

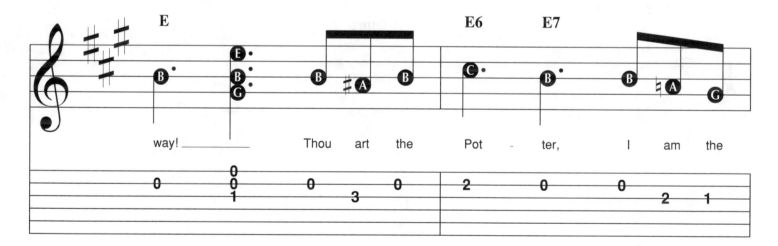

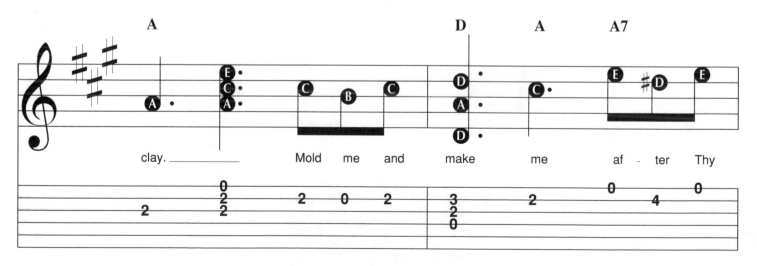

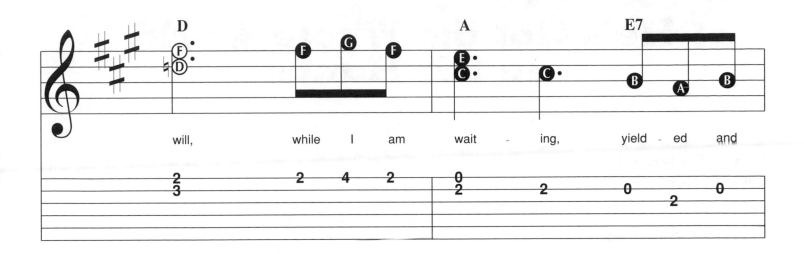

will,   while   I   am   wait - ing,   yield - ed   and

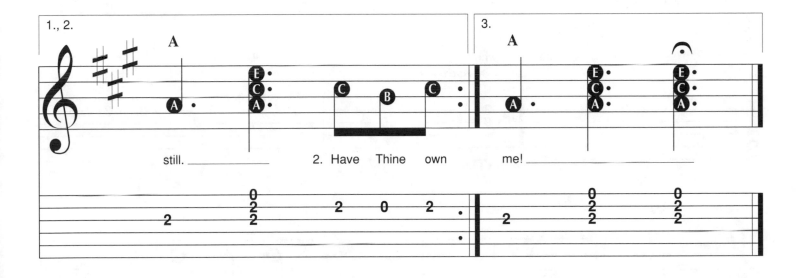

still. _____   2. Have   Thine   own   me! _____

Additional Lyrics

2. Have Thine own way, Lord! Have Thine own way!
   Search me and try me, Master, today!
   Whiter than snow, Lord, wash me just now,
   As in Thy presence humbly I bow.

3. Have Thine own way, Lord! Have Thine own way!
   Hold o'er my being absolute sway!
   Fill with Thy spirit till all shall see
   Christ only, always, living in me!

He's Got the Whole World in His Hands

African-American Folksong

Strum Pattern: 3, 4
Pick Pattern: 1, 3

1. He's got the whole world ____ in His hands, ____ He's got the
2., 3., 4. *See Additional Lyrics*

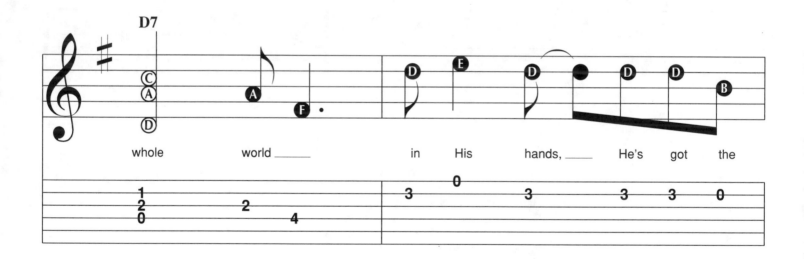

whole world ____ in His hands, ____ He's got the

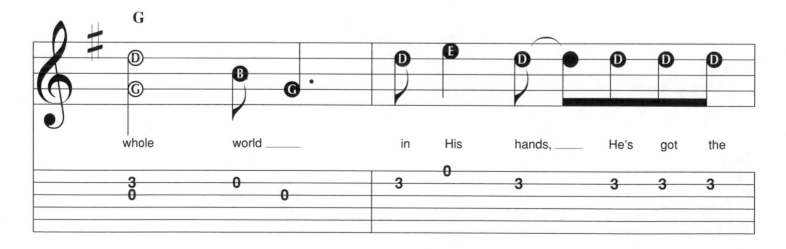

whole world ____ in His hands, ____ He's got the

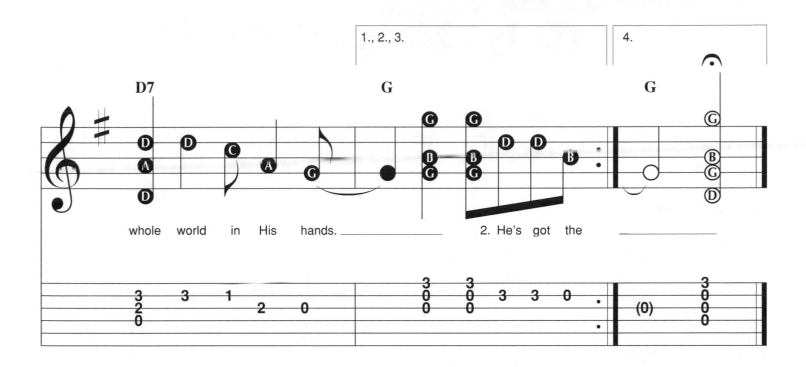

Additional Lyrics

2. He's got the wind and the rain in His hands,
   He's got the wind and the rain in His hands,
   He's got the wind and the rain in His hands,
   He's got the whole world in His hands.

3. He's got the tiny little baby in His hands,
   He's got the tiny little baby in His hands,
   He's got the tiny little baby in His hands,
   He's got the whole world in His hands.

4. He's got you and me, brother, in His hands,
   He's got you and me, sister, in His hands,
   He's got you and me, brother, in His hands,
   He's got the whole world in His hands.

Holy, Holy, Holy

Words by Reginald Heber
Music by John B. Dykes

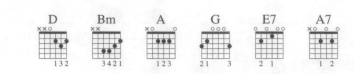

Strum Pattern: 3
Pick Pattern: 3

Verse
Joyfully

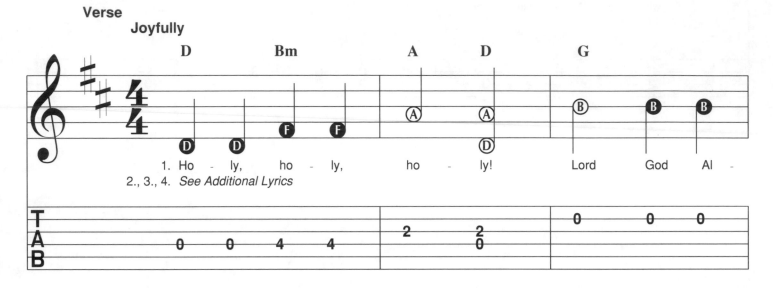

1. Ho - ly, ho - ly, ho - ly! Lord God Al -
2., 3., 4. *See Additional Lyrics*

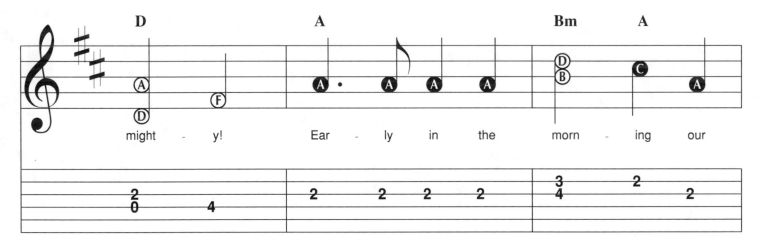

might - y! Ear - ly in the morn - ing our

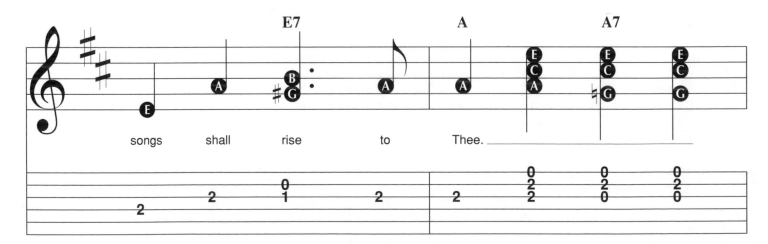

songs shall rise to Thee.

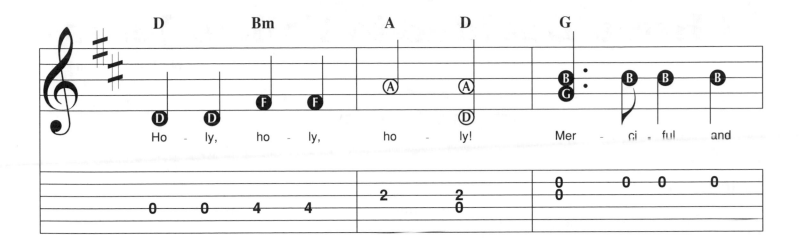

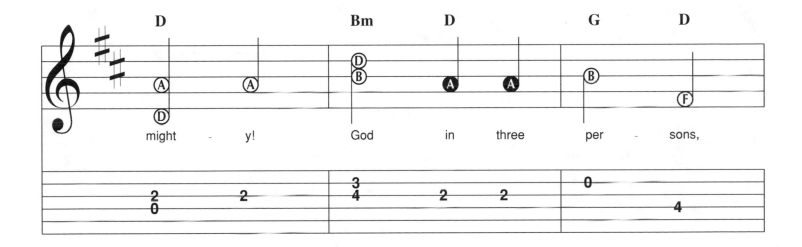

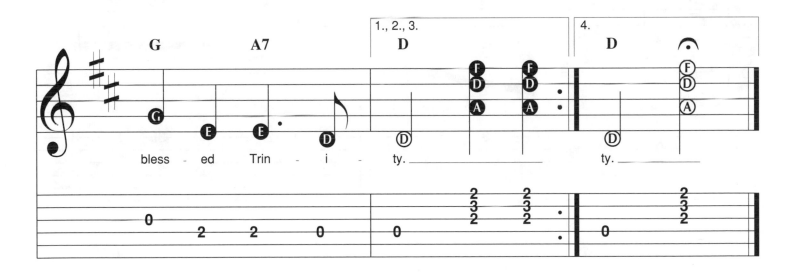

Additional Lyrics

2. Holy, holy, holy! All the saints adore Thee.
   Casting down their golden crowns around the glassy sea.
   Cherubim and seraphim falling down before Thee,
   Which wert, and art, and evermore shall be.

3. Holy, holy, holy! Through the darkness hide Thee.
   Through the eye of sinful man Thy glory may not see.
   Only Thou art holy; there is none beside Thee,
   Perfect in power, in love and purity.

4. Holy, holy, holy! Lord God Almighty!
   All Thy works shall praise Thy name in earth and sky and sea.
   Holy, holy, holy! Merciful and mighty!
   God in three persons, blessed Trinity.

I Have Decided to Follow Jesus

Words by an Indian Prince
Music by Auila Read

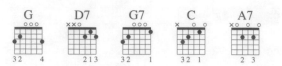

Strum Pattern: 6
Pick Pattern: 4

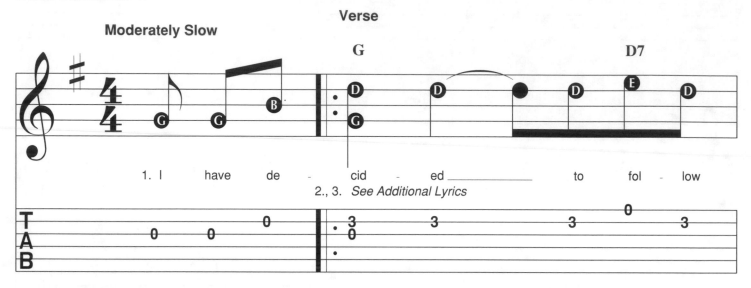

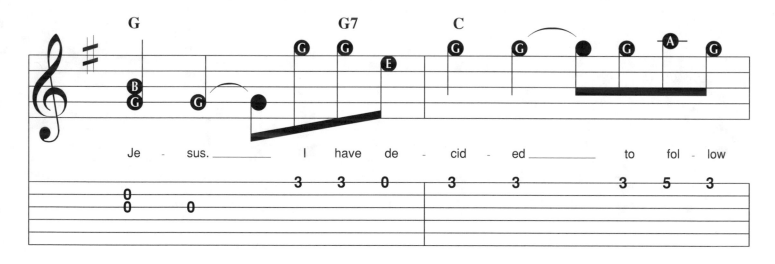

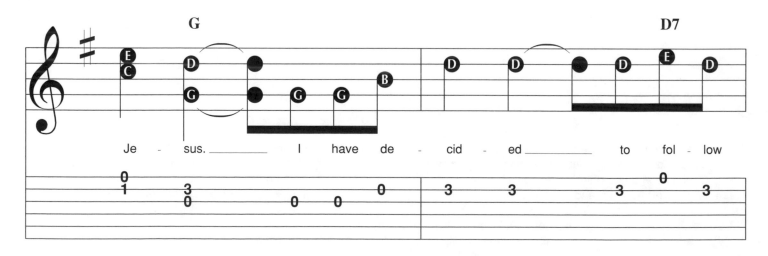

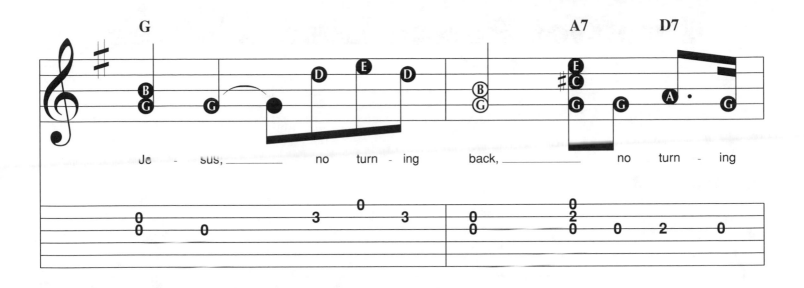

Je - sus, _____ no turn - ing back, _____ no turn - ing

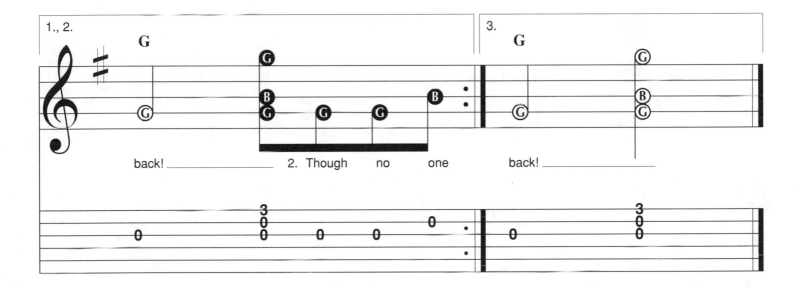

back! _____ 2. Though no one back! _____

Additional Lyrics

2. Though no one join me, still I will follow.
   Though no one join me, still I will follow.
   Though no one join me, still I will follow;
   No turning back, no turning back!

3. The world behind me, the cross before me;
   The world behind me, the cross before me;
   The world behind me, the cross before me;
   No turning back, no turning back!

I've Got Peace Like a River

Traditional

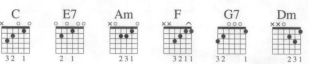

Strum Pattern: 3
Pick Pattern: 3

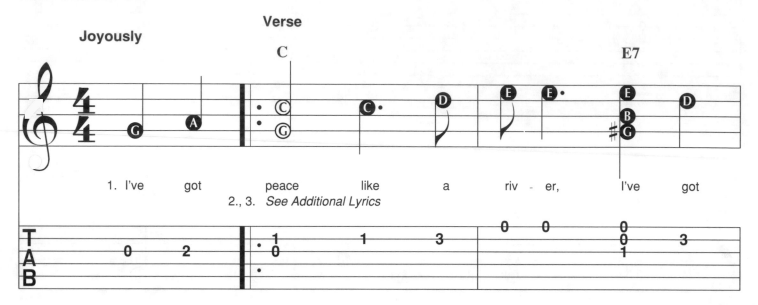

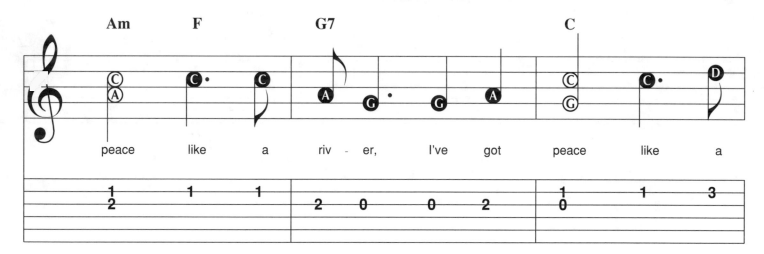

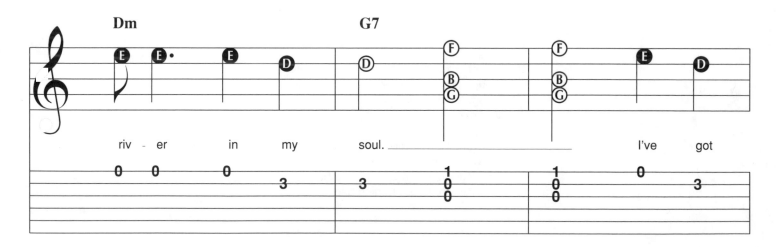

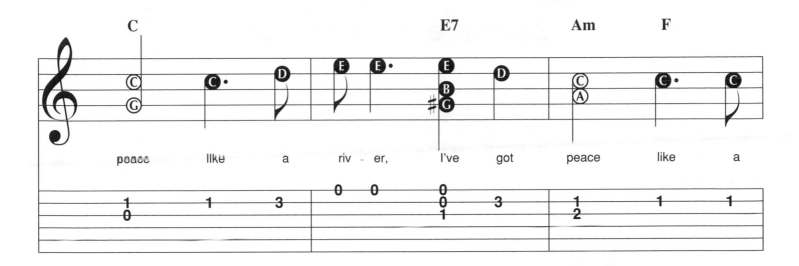

peace like a river, I've got peace like a

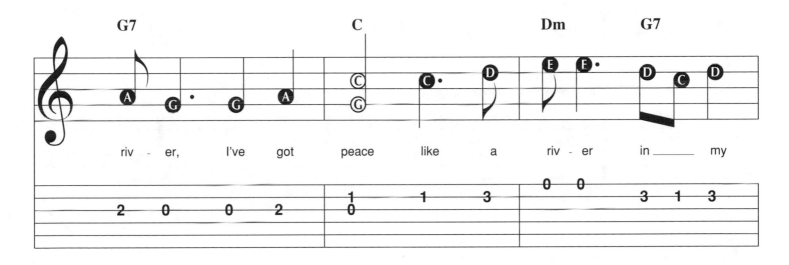

riv - er, I've got peace like a riv - er in _____ my

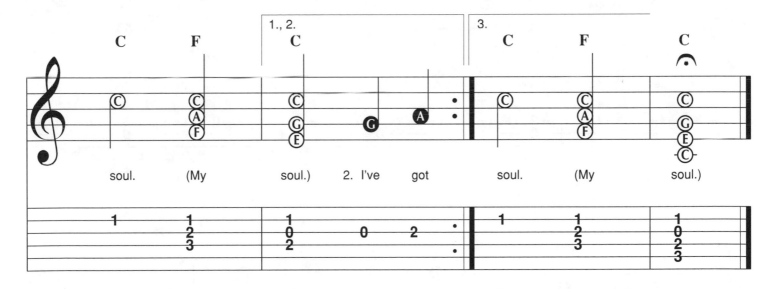

soul. (My soul.) 2. I've got soul. (My soul.)

Additional Lyrics

2. I've got love like an ocean,
   I've got love like an ocean,
   I've got love like an ocean in my soul.
   I've got love like an ocean,
   I've got love like an ocean,
   I've got love like an ocean in my soul. (My soul.)

3. I've got joy like a fountain,
   I've got joy like a fountain,
   I've got joy like a fountain in my soul.
   I've got joy like a fountain,
   I've got joy like a fountain,
   I've got joy like a fountain in my soul. (My soul.)

In the Garden

Words and Music by
C. Austin Miles

Strum Pattern: 8, 9
Pick Pattern: 8, 9

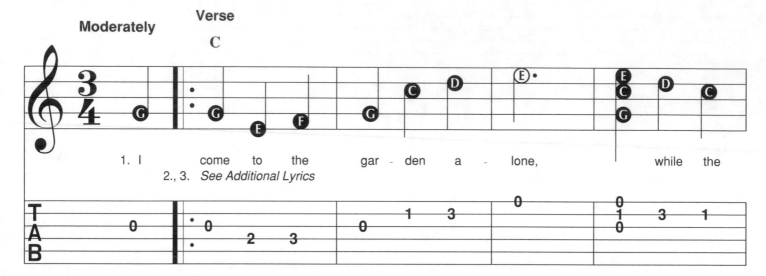

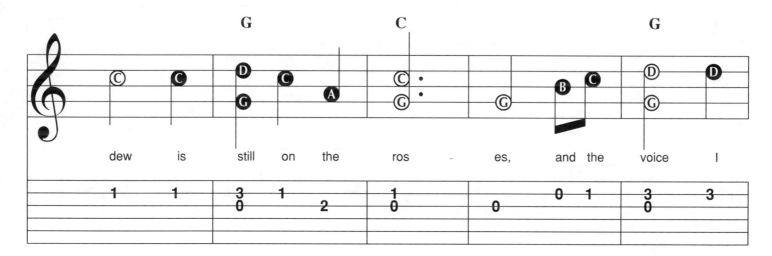

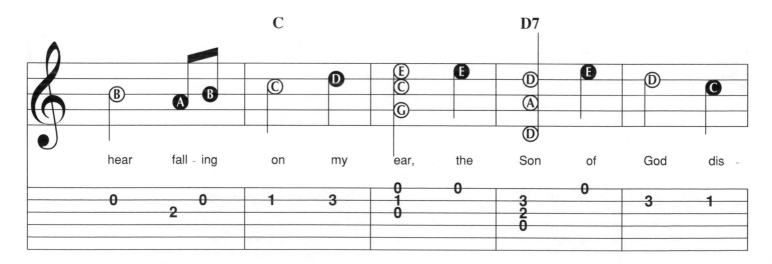

Copyright © 1999 by HAL LEONARD CORPORATION
International Copyright Secured   All Rights Reserved

40

Chorus

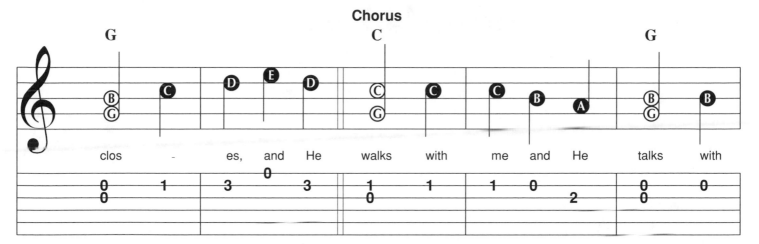

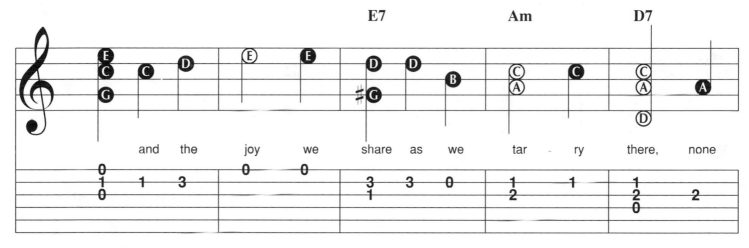

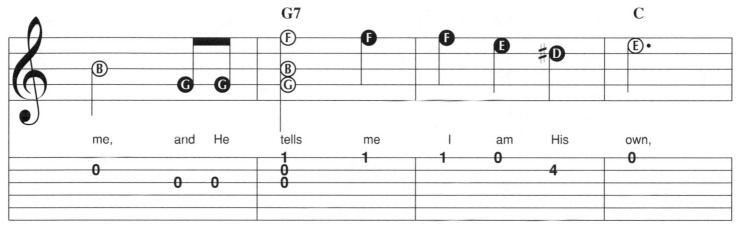

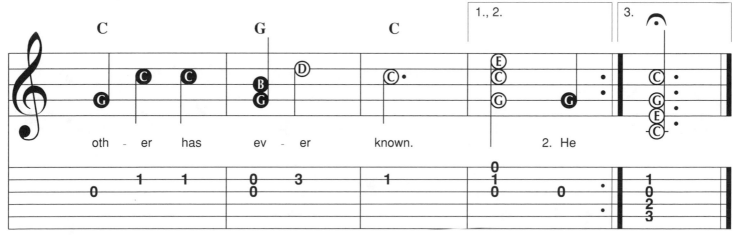

Additional Lyrics

2. He speaks, and the sound of His voice
   Is so sweet the birds hush their singing,
   And the melody that He gave to me
   Within my heart is ringing.

3. I'd stay in the garden with Him,
   Though the night around me be falling.
   But He bids me go through the voice of woe;
   His voice to me is calling.

Jacob's Ladder

African-American Spiritual

Strum Pattern: 8
Pick Pattern: 8

Verse
Soulfully

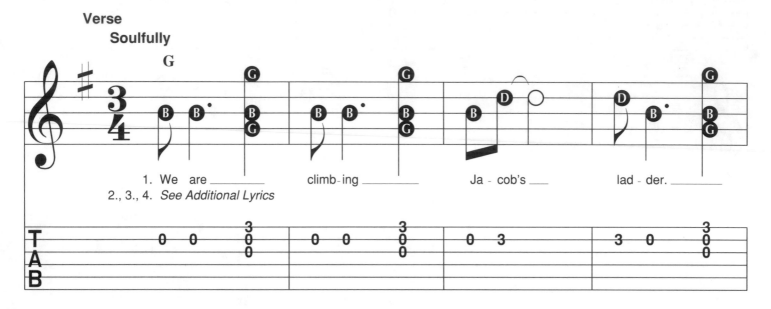

1. We are _____ climb-ing _____ Ja-cob's _____ lad-der.
2., 3., 4. *See Additional Lyrics*

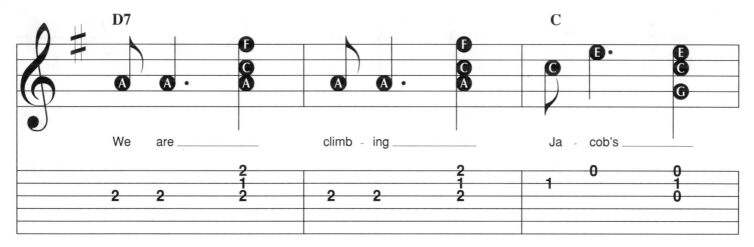

We are _____ climb-ing _____ Ja-cob's _____

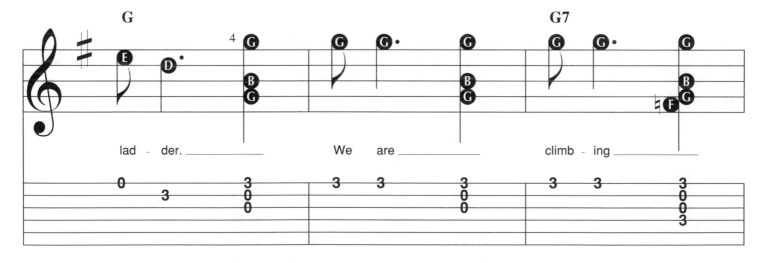

lad-der. _____ We are _____ climb-ing _____

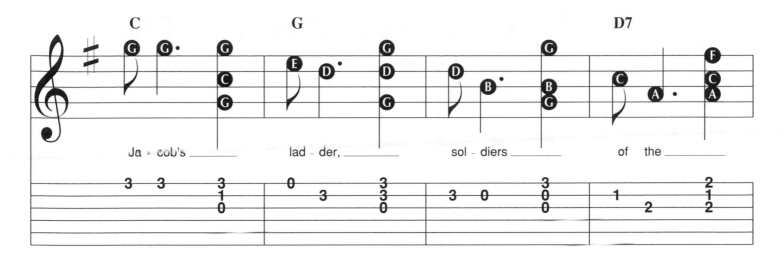

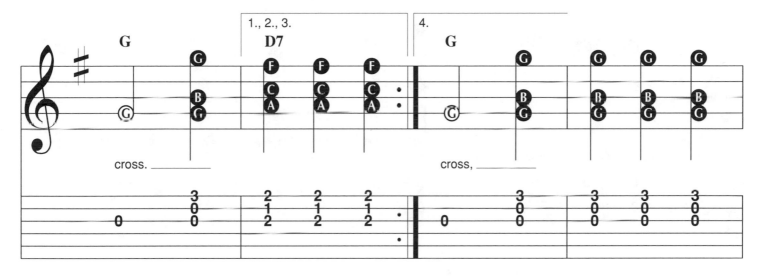

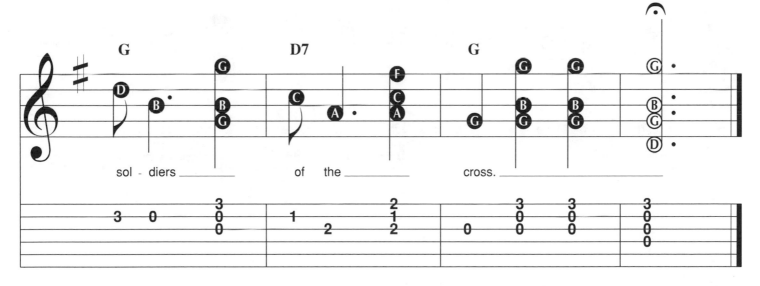

Additional Lyrics

2. Ev'ry round goes higher, higher.
   Ev'ry round goes higher, higher.
   Ev'ry round goes higher, higher,
   Soldiers of the cross.

3. We are climbing higher, higher.
   We are climbing higher, higher.
   We are climbing higher, higher,
   Soldiers of the cross.

4. If you love Him, why not serve Him?
   If you love Him, why not serve Him?
   If you love Him, why not serve Him?
   Soldiers of the cross,
   Soldiers of the cross,

Joyful, Joyful We Adore Thee

Words by Henry van Dyke
Music by Ludwig van Beethoven,
melody from Ninth Symphony
Adapted by Edward Hodges

Strum Pattern: 3
Pick Pattern: 4

Chorus
Moderately Fast

1. Joy - ful, joy - ful, we a - dore Thee, God of glo - ry,
2., 3. *See Additional Lyrics*

Lord of love; hearts un - fold like flowers be - fore Thee,

open - ing to the sun a - bove. Melt the clouds of

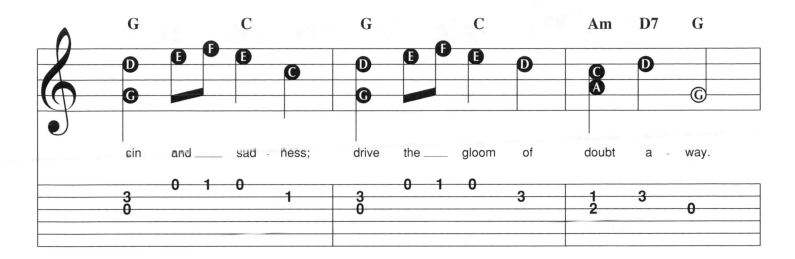

cin and ___ sad - ness; drive the ___ gloom of doubt a - way.

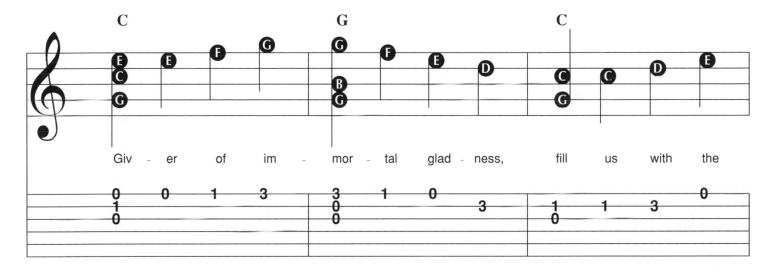

Giv - er of im - mor - tal glad - ness, fill us with the

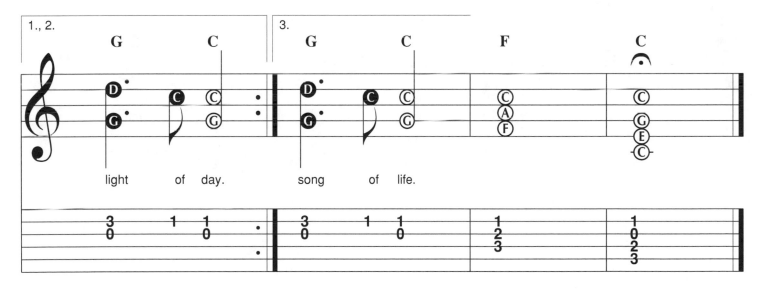

light of day.   song of life.

Additional Lyrics

2. All Thy works with joy surround Thee,
Earth and heaven reflect Thy rays.
Stars and angels sing around Thee,
Center of unbroken praise.
Field and forest, vale and mountain,
Flowery meadow, flashing sea,
Chanting bird and flowing fountain,
Call us to rejoice in Thee.

3. Mortals, join the happy chorus
Which the morning stars began.
Love devine is reigning o'er us,
Joining all in heaven's plan.
Ever singing, march we onward,
Victors in the midst of strife.
Joyful music leads us sunward,
In the triumph song of life.

Let Us Break Bread Together

African-American Spiritual

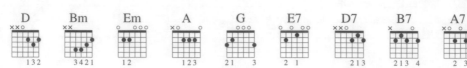

Strum Pattern: 3
Pick Pattern: 3

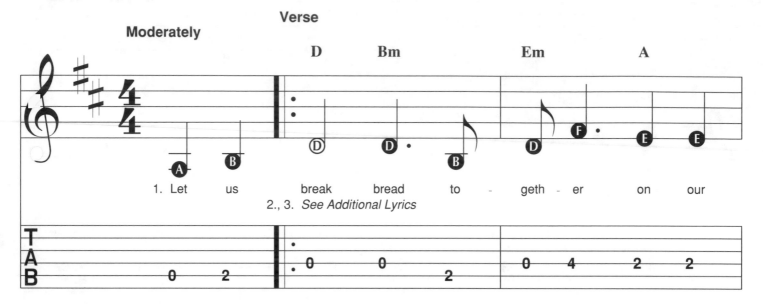

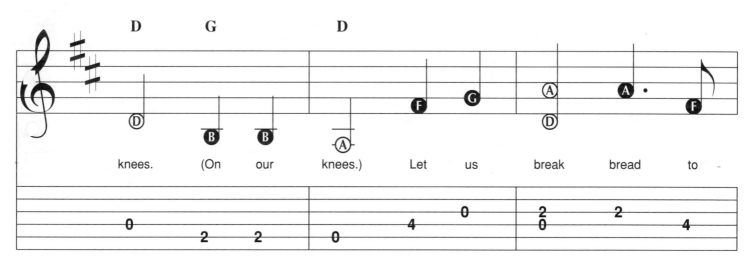

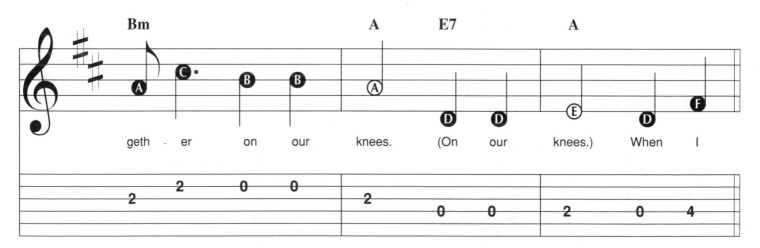

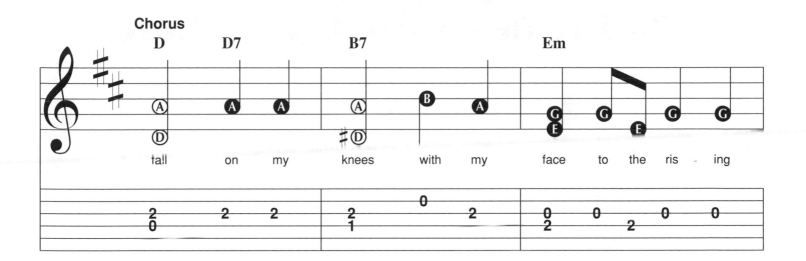

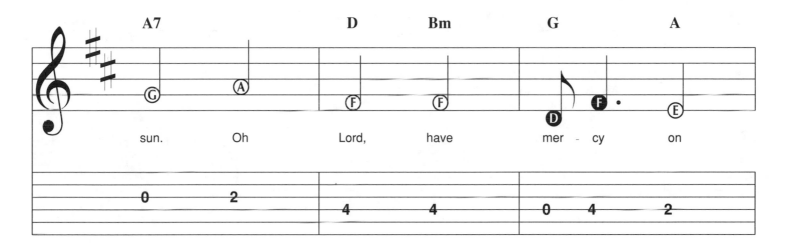

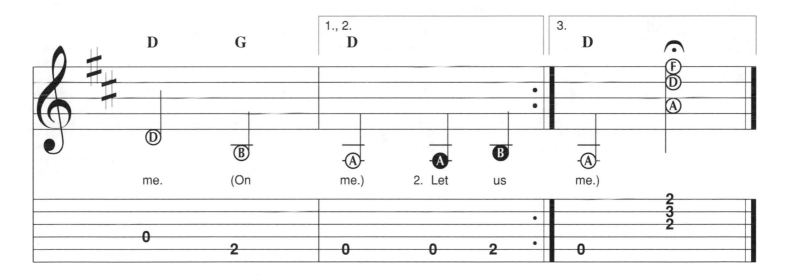

Additional Lyrics

2. Let us drink the cup together on our knees.
   (On our knees.)
   Let us drink the cup together on our knees.
   (On our knees.)

3. Let us praise God together on our knees.
   (On our knees.)
   Let us praise God together on our knees.
   (On our knees.)

My Faith Looks Up to Thee

Words by Ray Palmer
Music by Lowell Mason

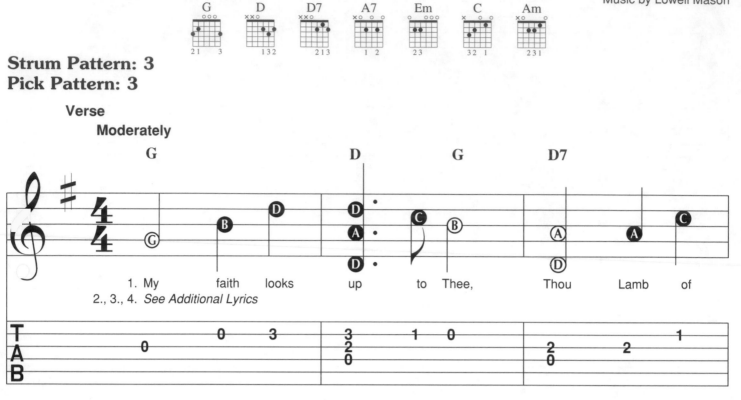

Strum Pattern: 3
Pick Pattern: 3

Verse
Moderately

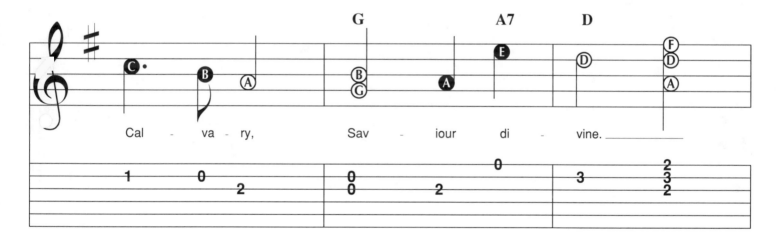

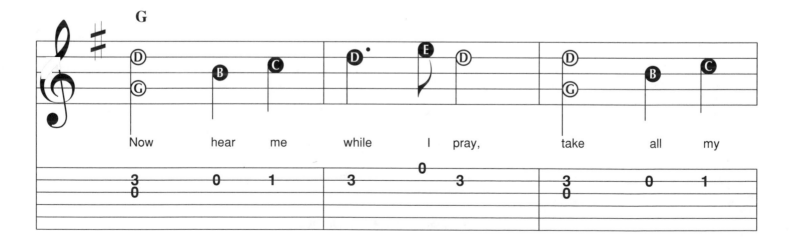

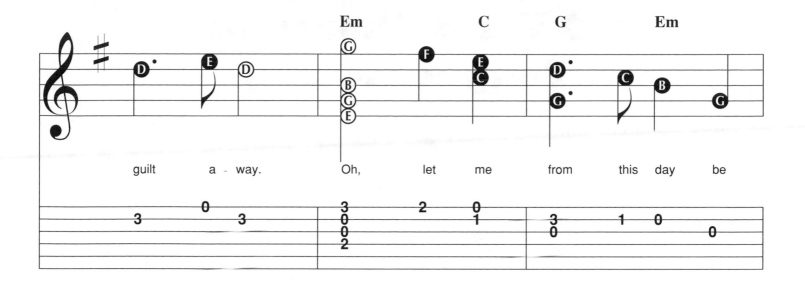

guilt a - way. Oh, let me from this day be

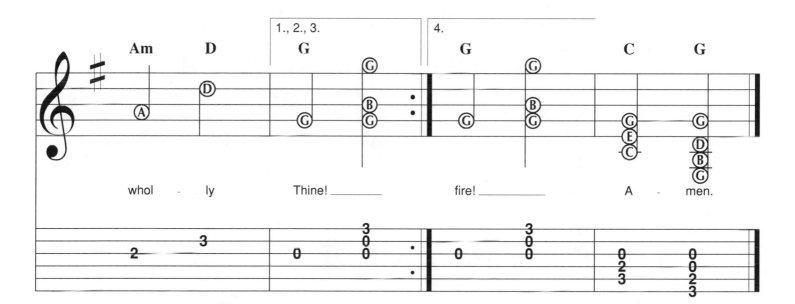

whol - ly Thine! _____ fire! _____ A - men.

Additional Lyrics

2. When ends life's transient dream,
   When death's cold, sullen stream
   Shall o'er me roll,
   Blest Saviour, then, in love,
   Fear and distrust remove.
   Oh bear me safe above,
   A ransomed soul!

3. While life's dark maze I tread,
   And griefs around me spread,
   Be Thou my guide.
   Bid darkness turn to day,
   Wipe sorrow's tears away.
   Nor let me ever stray
   From Thee aside.

4. May Thy rich grace impart
   Strength to my fainting heart,
   My zeal inspire.
   As Thou has died for me,
   Oh may my love to Thee,
   Pure, warm, and changeless by,
   A living fire! Amen.

O For a Thousand Tongues to Sing

Text by Charles Wesley
Music by Carl G. Glaser

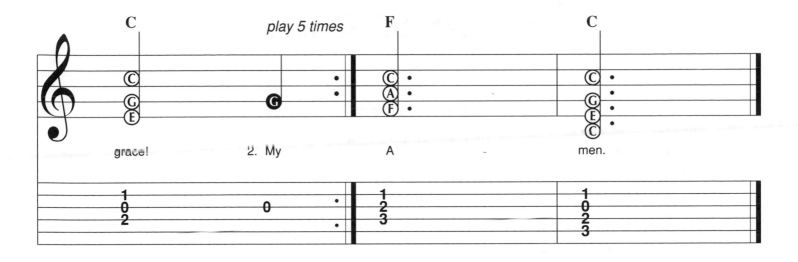

Additional Lyrics

2. My gracious Master and my God,
   Assist me to proclaim,
   To spread through all the earth abroad
   The honors of Thy name.

3. Jesus! The name that charms our fears,
   That bids our sorrows cease,
   'Tis music in the sinner's ears,
   'Tis life and health and peace.

4. He breaks the pow'r of canceled sin,
   He sets the prisoner free;
   His blood can make the foulest clean,
   His blood availed for me.

5. Hear Him, ye deaf, His praise, ye dumb,
   Your loosened tongues employ;
   Ye blind, behold your Savior come,
   And leap, ye lame, for joy! Amen.

Rock of Ages

Text by Augustus M. Toplady
Music by Thomas Hastings

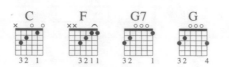

Strum Pattern: 8
Pick Pattern: 8

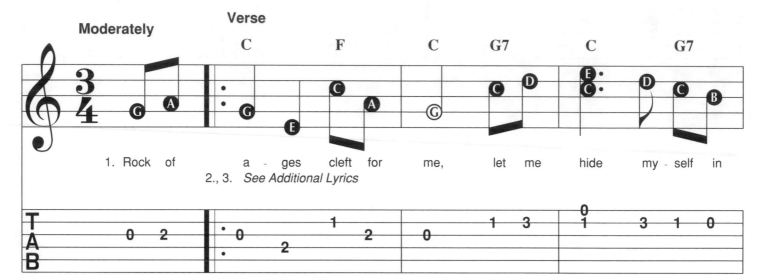

1. Rock of a - ges cleft for me, let me hide my - self in

2., 3. *See Additional Lyrics*

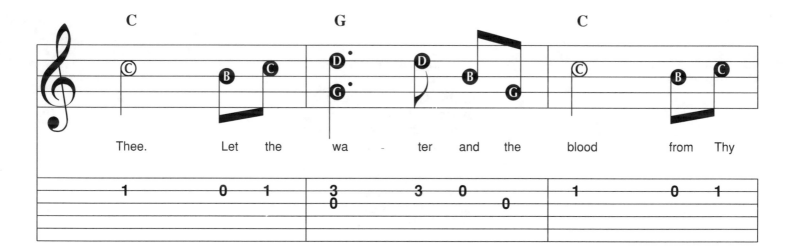

Thee. Let the wa - ter and the blood from Thy

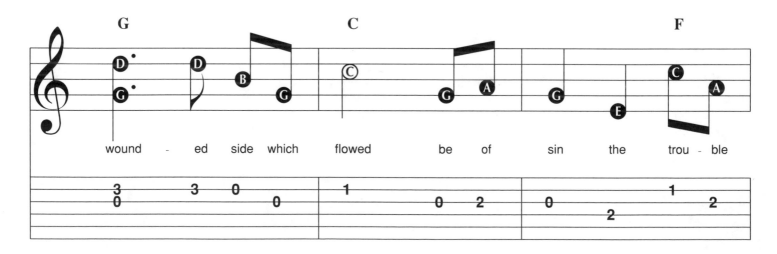

wound - ed side which flowed be of sin the trou - ble

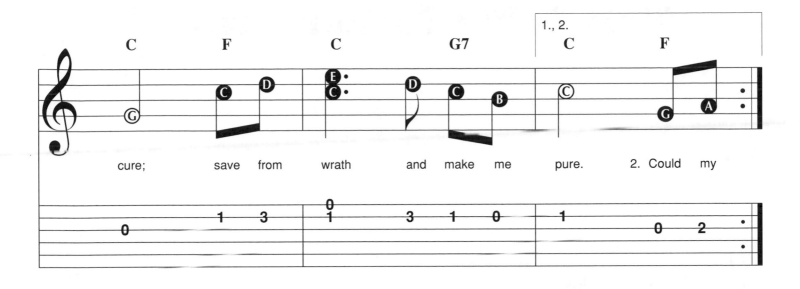

cure;　　save from　wrath　　and　make　me　pure.　2. Could　my

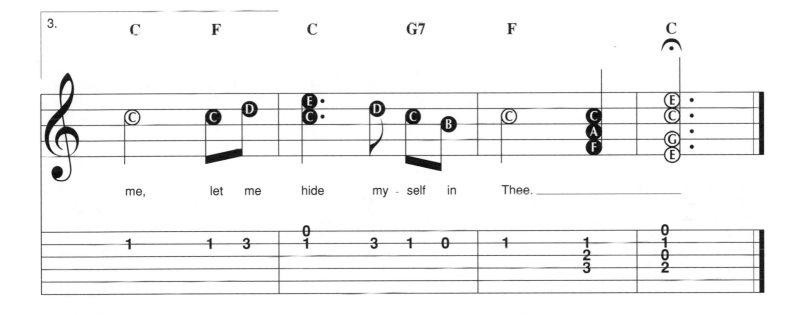

me,　　let　me　hide　my - self　in　Thee. _____

Additional Lyrics

2. Could my tears forever flow,
   Could my zeal no langour know?
   These for sin could not atone,
   Thou must save and Thou alone.
   In my hand no price I bring,
   Simply to Thy cross I cling.

3. While I draw this fleeting breath,
   When my eyes shall close in death.
   When I rise to worlds unknown,
   And behold Thee on Thy throne.
   Rock of ages cleft for me,
   Let me hide myself in Thee.

This Is My Father's World

Words by Maltbie Babcock
Music by Franklin L. Sheppard

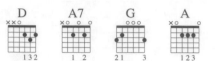

Strum Pattern: 2
Pick Pattern: 2

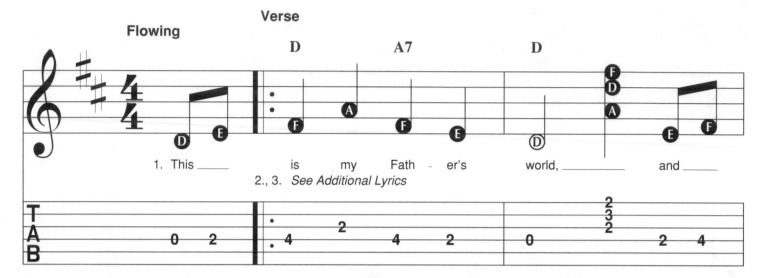

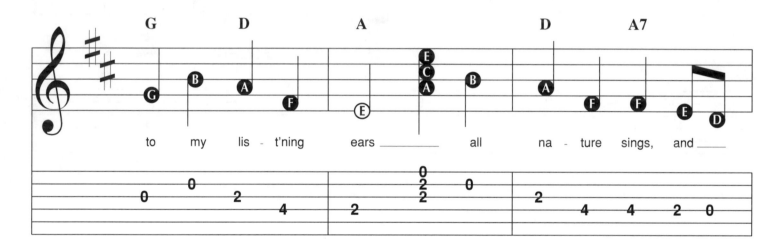

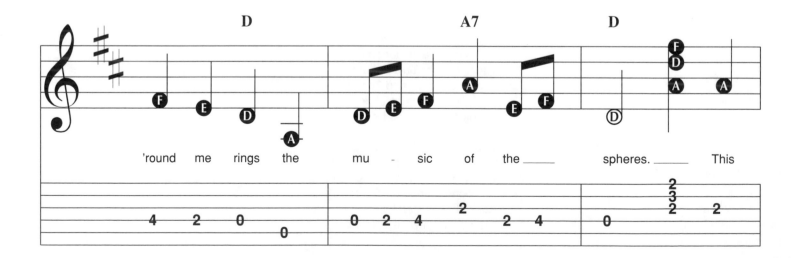

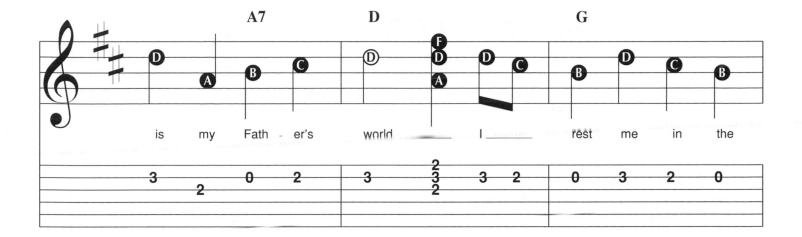

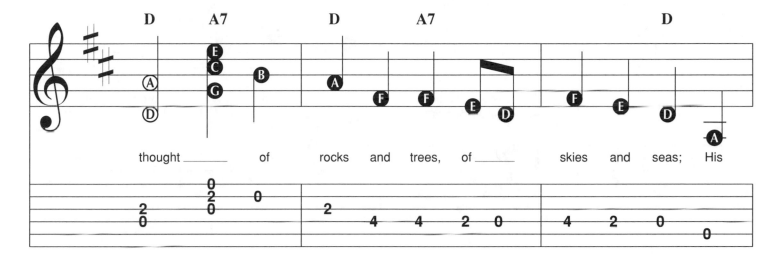

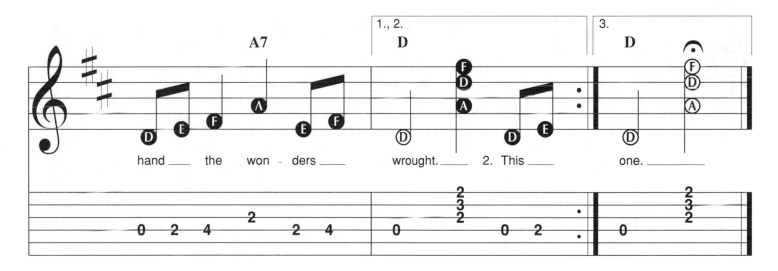

Additional Lyrics

2. This is my Father's world, the birds their carrols raise.
   The morning light, the lily white, declare their maker's praise.
   This is my Father's world, He shines in all that's fair.
   In the rustling grass I hear Him pass, He speaks to me everywhere.

3. This is my Father's world, oh let me ne'er forget
   That though the wrong seems oft so strong, God is the Ruler yet.
   This is my Father's world, the battle is not done.
   Jesus who died shall be satisfied, and earth and heav'n be one.

Were You There?

African-American Spiritual
Harmony by Charles Winfred Douglas

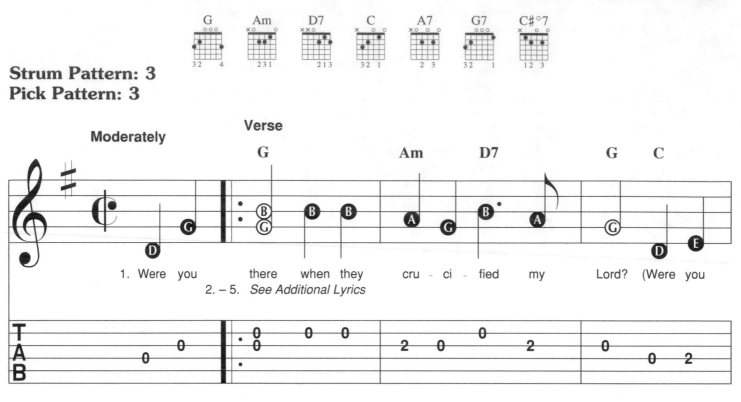

Strum Pattern: 3
Pick Pattern: 3

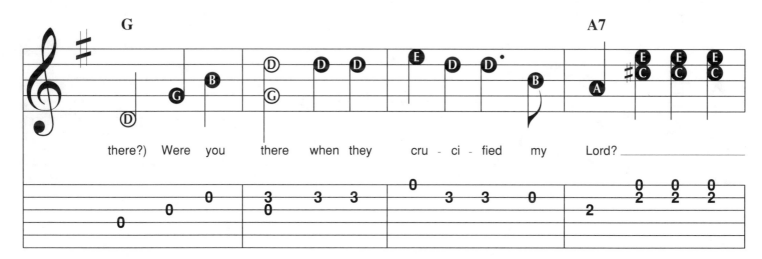

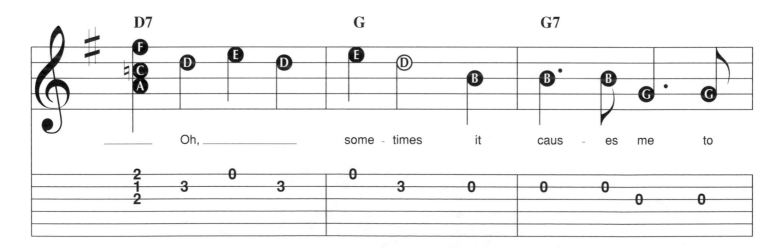

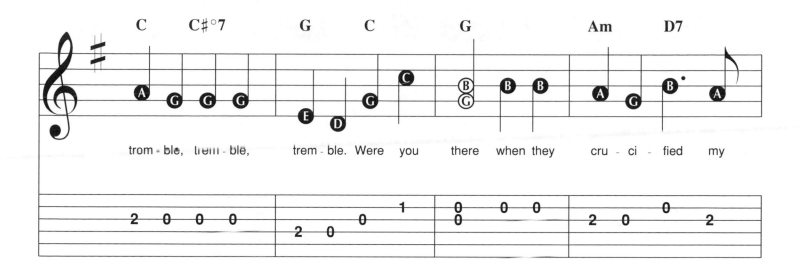

trem-ble, trem-ble, trem-ble. Were you there when they cru - ci - fied my

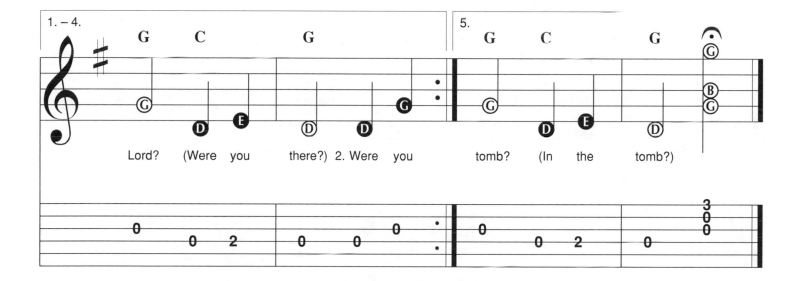

Lord? (Were you there?) 2. Were you tomb? (In the tomb?)

Additional Lyrics

2. Were you there when they nailed Him to the tree? (To the tree?)
   Were you there when they nailed Him to the tree? (To the tree?)
   Oh, sometimes it causes me to tremble, tremble, tremble.
   Were you there when they nailed Him to the tree? (To the tree?)

3. Were you there when they pierced Him in the side? (In the side?)
   Were you there when they pierced Him in the side? (In the side?)
   Oh, sometimes it causes me to tremble, tremble, tremble.
   Were you there when they pierced Him in the side? (In the side?)

4. Were you there when the sun refused to shine? (Were you there?)
   Were you there when the sun refused to shine? (Were you there?)
   Oh, sometimes it causes me to tremble, tremble, tremble.
   Were you there when the sun refused to shine? (Were you there?)

5. Were you there when they laid Him in the tomb? (In the tomb?)
   Were you there when they laid Him in the tomb? (In the tomb?)
   Oh, sometimes it causes me to tremble, tremble, tremble.
   Were you there when they laid Him in the tomb? (In the tomb?)

What a Friend We Have in Jesus

Words by Joseph Scriven
Music by Charles C. Converse

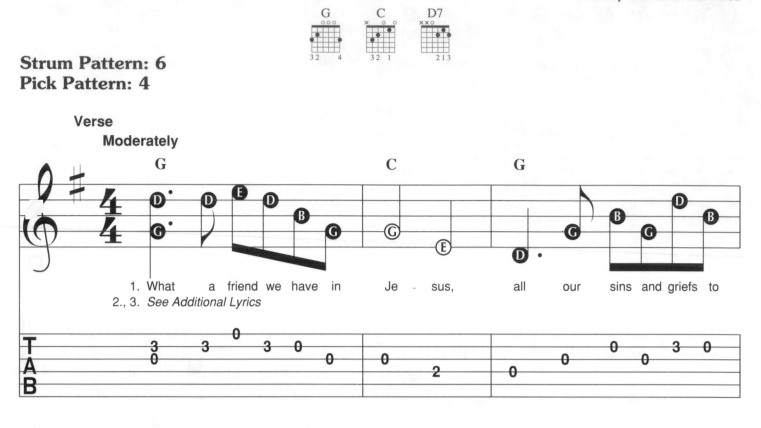

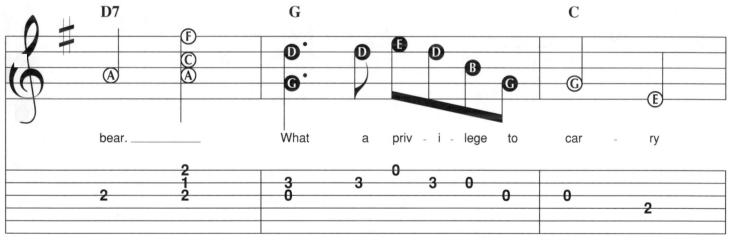

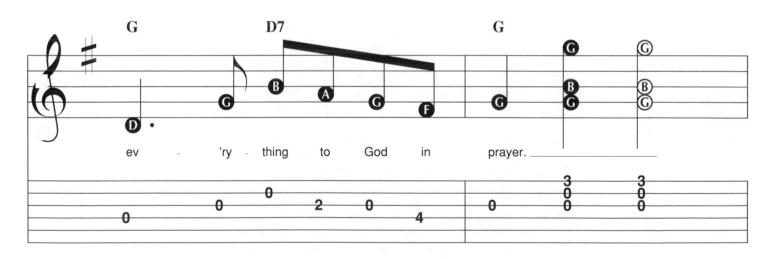

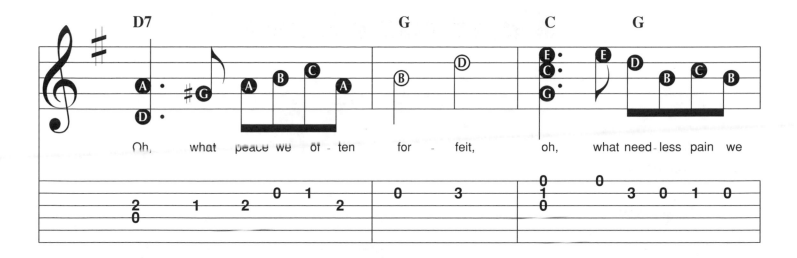

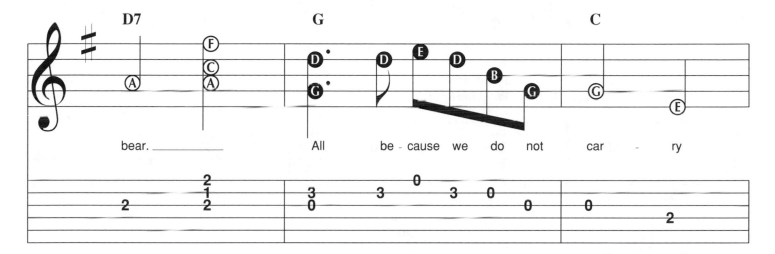

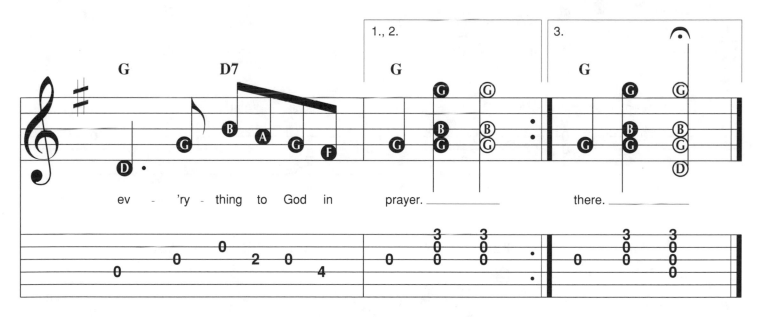

Additional Lyrics

2. Have we trials and temptations,
   Is there troubles anywhere?
   We should never be discouraged;
   Take it to the Lord in prayer.
   Can we find a friend so faithful
   Who will all our sorrows share?
   Jesus knows our ev'ry weakness;
   Take it to the Lord in prayer.

3. Are we weak and heavy laden,
   Cumbered with a load of care?
   Precious Savior still our refuge;
   Take it to the Lord in prayer.
   Do thy friends despise, forsake thee?
   Take it to the Lord in prayer.
   In His arms He'll take and shield thee;
   Thou will find a solice there.

Wondrous Love

Southern American Folk Hymn

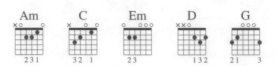

Strum Pattern: 4
Pick Pattern: 6

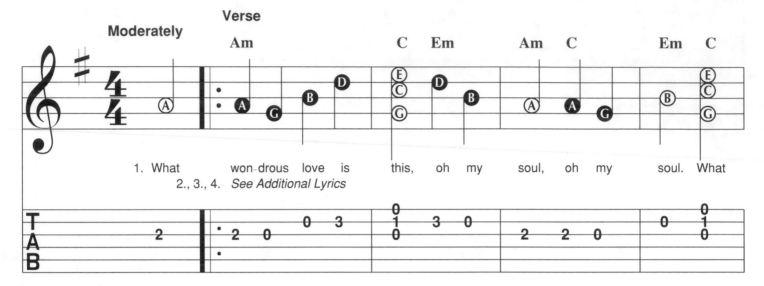

1. What won-drous love is this, oh my soul, oh my soul. What
2., 3., 4. *See Additional Lyrics*

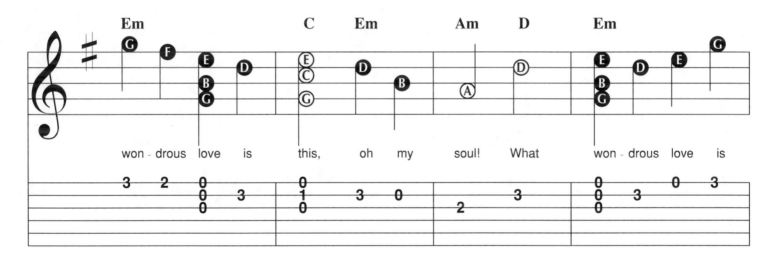

won - drous love is this, oh my soul! What won - drous love is

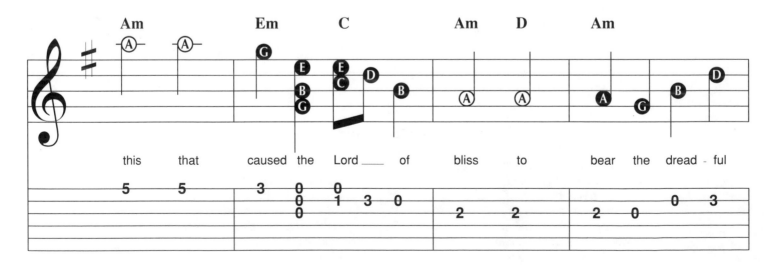

this that caused the Lord ___ of bliss to bear the dread - ful

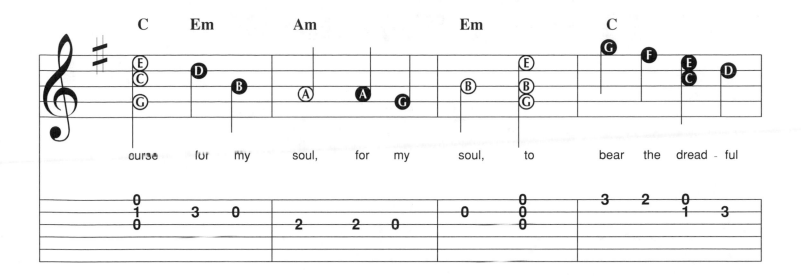

curse for my soul, for my soul, to bear the dread - ful

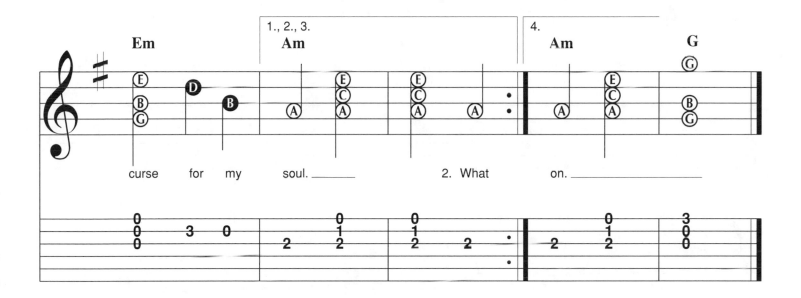

curse for my soul. _____ 2. What on. _____

Additional Lyrics

2. What wondrous love is this, oh my soul, oh my soul.
   What wondrous love is this, oh my soul!
   What wondrous love is this that caused the Lord of life
   To lay aside His crown for my soul, for my soul,
   To lay aside His crown for my soul!

3. To God and to the Lamb I will sing, I will sing,
   To God and to the Lamb I will sing.
   To God and to the Lamb who is the great AM,
   While millions join the theme I will sing, I will sing,
   While millions join the theme I will sing.

4. And when from death I'm free, I'll sing on, I'll sing on,
   And when from death I'm free, I'll sing on.
   And when from death I'm free, I'll sing and joyful be,
   And through eternity I'll sing on, I'll sing on,
   And through eternity I'll sing on.

I Love to Tell the Story

Words by A. Catherine Hankey
Music by William G. Fischer

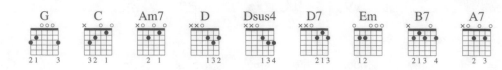

Strum Pattern: 4
Pick Pattern: 4

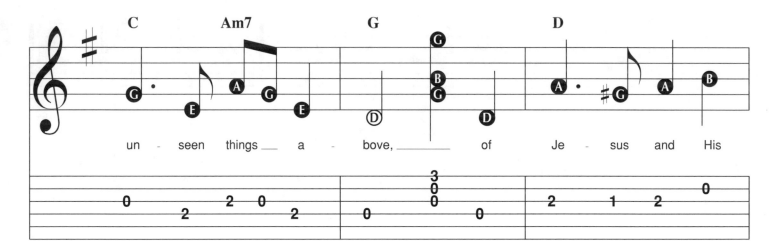

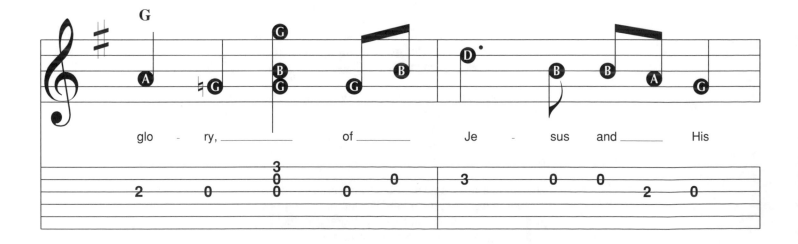

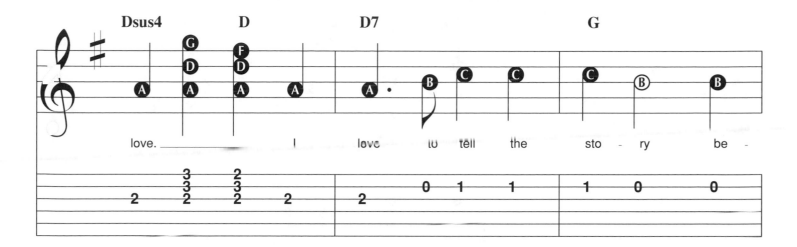

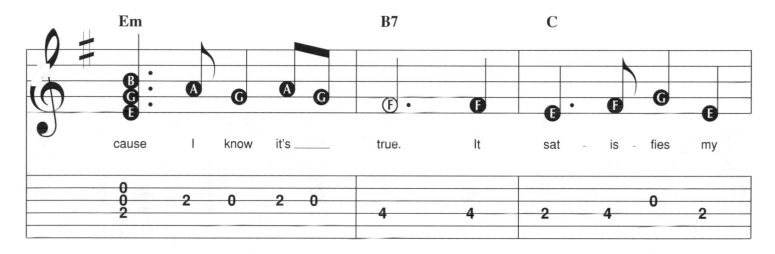

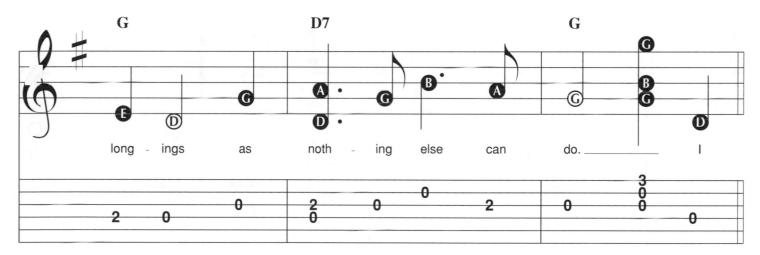

Chorus

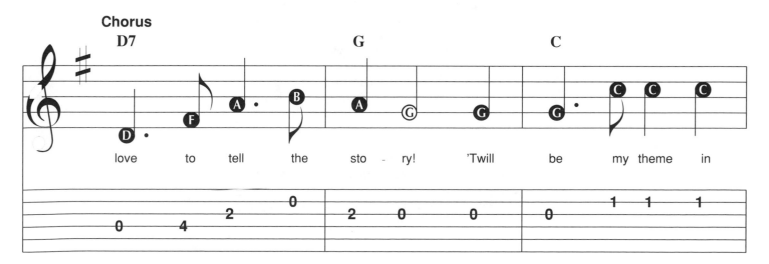

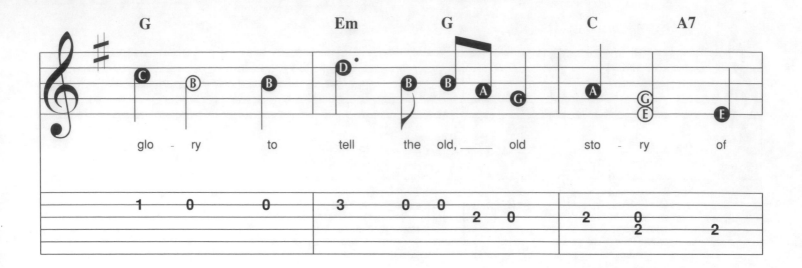

glo - ry   to   tell   the   old,____ old   sto - ry   of

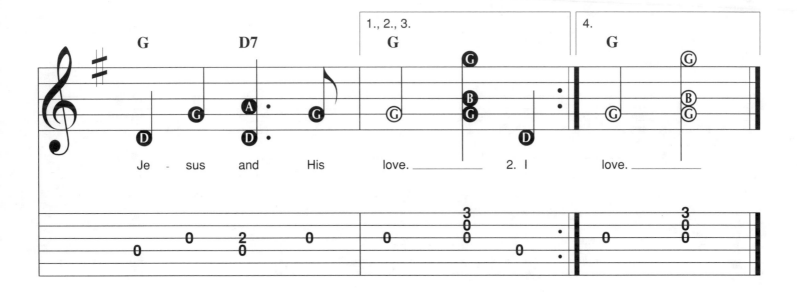

Je - sus   and   His   love.____   2. I   love.____

Additional Lyrics

2. I love to tell the story; more wonderful it seems
   Than all the golden fancies of all our golden dreams.
   I love to tell the story; it did so much for me,
   And that is just the reason I tell it now to thee.

3. I love to tell the story, 'tis pleasant to repeat.
   What seems each time I tell it, more wonderfully sweet.
   I love to tell the story for some have never heard
   The message of salvation from God's own holy word.

4. I love to tell the story; for those who know it best
   Seem hungering and thirsting to hear it like the rest.
   And when, in scenes of glory, I sing the new, new song,
   'Twill be the old, old story that I have loved so long.